IN AND OUT THE WINDOWS

IN AND OUT THE WINDOWS:

My life as a Psychic

Dilys Gater

Chivers Press • Thorndike Press
Bath, England • Thorndike, Maine USA

B GATER

VL Lt

This Large Print edition is published by Chivers Press, England, and by Thorndike Press, USA.

Published in 2001 in the U.K. by arrangement with the author.

Published in 2001 in the U.S. by arrangement with Dilys Gater.

U.K. Hardcover ISBN 0–7540–4330–4 (Chivers Large Print)
U.K. Softcover ISBN 0–7540–4331–2 (Camden Large Print)
U.S. Softcover ISBN 0–7862–3026–6 (General Series Edition)

The text of this Large Print edition is unabridged.
Other aspects of the book may vary from the original edition.

Set in 16 pt. New Times Roman.

Printed in Great Britain on acid-free paper.

British Library Cataloguing in Publication Data available

Library of Congress Control Number: 00–092642

For Paul
in celebration of the known and the unknown

For DHS and for Richard
in gratitude for light on my path

For Geraldine, Micola and Rosemarie
to thank them for being my friends

And in tribute to Chokecherry Gall Eagle
who wrote
'I thank my enemies, and laugh;
you have only made me stronger.'

CONTENTS

INTRODUCTION

In and out the windows
In and out the windows
In and out the windows
As you have done before

These are the words of a children's game I can remember playing in the village school when I was growing up in North Wales. What do they mean? As with most such children's games, they are traditional and inscrutable—children never bother about meanings, they are too wise for that. The games go on, the ancient rituals are performed even if their significance is lost in race memory, touchstones through the generations for what it is to be human and to be alive.

Life as a psychic has something of this quality. When people learn that I am 'second sighted', that I practise as a psychic and healer, they often comment that it must be disconcerting—frightening, even—to be able to look into the future, or to live in close awareness of the presence of spirits and beings the average person does not expect to encounter every day. Life as a psychic is generally assumed to be extremely spooky, not at all like the life led by people who work in banking, catering, plumbing or similarly

1

respectable trades.

In fact, though, possessing the ability to pass through all the mystical and esoteric complexities of being a psychic seems, to the person who is gifted with 'the sight', just as simple and natural as a child being able to pass 'in and out the windows' of an imaginative game. As children, we were all able to do this to some extent for the young, as well as the very old, are closer to the boundaries of living—the past and the future, the acceptances and beliefs that would-be-sophisticated souls are inclined to disregard or even dismiss in their progress through a full and energetic life in the material world.

Being able to live on many planes, the spiritual as well as the physical, in the past and the future as well as the present; being able to 'read' people's inmost thoughts and hopes and fears; being in communication with the worlds of the dead, of animals and elemental spirits and angels, with the realms of Guides and Gatekeepers—as well as some of the rather less elevated beings one can encounter—this is no different in practical terms to being able to travel among the varied peoples, countries and continents of the world we all know, and finding that there are great wonders to be discovered, much to be learned.

In this book I have tried to give some idea of what my life as a psychic involves. Each chapter roughly represents one of its many aspects, 'windows' through which I might pass, both in and out, in the course of any day in my own meditations and experience or when dealing with the people who consult me. Psychic awareness is actually a natural state— it is simply our own refusal to accept (with our rational brains and insistence on tangible proof) that 'there is more in heaven and earth, Horatio, than is dreamed of in your philosophy', that gets in the way.

I like to think that the answer to all the great problems that face us today might be simply glimpsed in the image of everyone being willing to unite once more in a kind of cosmic 'play', to return to the child's acceptance of things it may not understand but simply feel with its heart, and to link hands and pass 'in and out the windows' together.

DILYS GATER

CHAPTER ONE

WHAT DO YOU DO?

This is the question I am most often asked
when people learn I am a psychic. My business
card actually states: 'Clairvoyance—Medium—
Tarot—Healer.' But as to what I actually *do* in
the course of my work, this can vary from
simply listening to the problems of sitters and
helping them to see that they have a choice of
ways forward, to the most dramatic kind of
'ghost-busting'. I find I am called on to
undertake the most unexpected, sometimes
daunting tasks.

Apparently simple problems have been
known to turn into cases involving demonic
possession or requiring a house to be 'cleared'
of invasion by elemental spirits. But on the
other hand sitters who have consulted me in
desperation, thinking they were going mad or
that their lives had been ruined for ever, may
have needed only to be reassured that they
were unaware of their own depths of psychic
or spiritual power. As with all spiritual calling
and vocation however, I have never yet been
faced with anything that was beyond my
strength, even though it might have seemed
bewilderingly so at the time.

I came to awareness of my psychic gifts relatively late in life, though looking back there were clear indications that I was 'second sighted' right from the start, if anyone had been able to read them. Unfortunately nobody did, so rather than being advised on how to use my powers wisely and develop them in order to proceed on my own spiritual path, I spent many years trying to fit into a world that seemed very difficult to me, and I was often ill.

The illnesses were variously diagnosed as 'nervous breakdowns' or mental imbalance of different kinds, but I can see now that they were probably caused by my inability to recognise that many of my experiences and awarenesses were on different mental and spiritual planes to the physical. I learned later how to protect myself against the depletion and exhaustion that so many times landed me in hospital. Psychics call it 'burn-out' and it is one of the hazards of possessing psychic power that is not properly handled.

But everything is there for a purpose. Once I began to realise that I was not mentally ill or 'mad' and learned to have faith in my own conviction of reality and my own sense of truth, I could see that all the trials of the past, including my spells in psychiatric hospitals and my struggles to come to terms with life and the great mysteries beyond it, made sense. If I had not had those painful experiences myself I would not have been able to draw on them to offer practical support and understanding to the people who consult me now.

So many times, whether the problem is a spiritual crisis or some messy emotional tangle in the 'real' world, it seems to give sitters comfort and confidence if I can tell them I have been through the experience myself and have some idea of what they must be feeling and suffering.

I am called on to give advice on philosophies of living and spiritual counsel as well as divining what the future will hold, conducting past life regression sessions, laying out the Tarot cards, reading people's palms, and the many other activities which are more commonly believed to make up the daily life of someone who works in this field. In actual fact, though, what I really 'do' is to try as sincerely as I can to follow my own spiritual path in my daily living—whether I can help others along the way is something that is granted as an extra bonus.

My psychic career began in my early forties when it seemed that I had already lived a very full life and could ask for little more to happen that would not be an anti-climax. I had been successful in my chosen sphere of work and managed to keep myself in business as a writer and novelist, with more than sixty books published. I had been married three times, had a grown-up daughter and had also experienced one long-standing and passionate love affair which had shaped my professional and personal existence and which I would never forget. Though I was now footloose and broke, had recently undergone three surgical operations, was living alone in a tiny studio flat in London, in poor health and finding it hard to make ends meet, I still considered I had had a good life, better than most.

It was at this point, when I had begun to wonder whether perhaps the best part of my life was over, that my psychic gift—the fact that I was 'second sighted'—was revealed to me. I had always been interested in philosophies and the religions of different cultures though never, I would have said, overtly spiritual. And I had had no contact whatsoever with the world of psychics, except that twice when times had been very bad I had in desperation visited a local lady who read my Tarot cards. Her reassurances helped me very much, and she told me that I had psychic powers—a statement that seemed so incredible I was not prepared to believe it.

But looking round for something to hold onto and give me hope in the area of London where I was now living and where I was a relative stranger, I was drawn to the nearby Spiritualist Church. Previously I had been inclined—along with most people who know nothing about such matters—to regard the activities of mediums as, if not rather suspect, then amusingly eccentric and 'all in the mind'. I had in fact played the part of Madame Arcati in Noel Coward's *Blithe Spirit* on the amateur stage some years before, which later seemed quite a coincidence—though of course, there are no coincidences in the spirit world.

I found that attending services at the Spiritualist Church brought me new understanding and peace of mind. I was at last among people who did not regard my perceptions of reality or my values as unreal. But rather to my discomfiture I discovered that though I considered myself a newcomer, a beginner if you like, wanting to learn from those more experienced and wiser than I, nevertheless I seemed to be intuitively aware of many things that suggested I was no learner. I found I had an unexpected grasp and knowledge of many extremely deep and complex spiritual truths, as well as psychic and mediumistic powers.

One of the most difficult things for 'new' or aspiring psychics to accept is that though they might regard themselves as basically just ordinary, they could find themselves overnight, as it were, performing seemingly amazing psychic feats. They have to learn to trust their inspiration and ability, to have confidence in their spiritual destiny.

I was no exception. At one moment it seemed I had been helpless and struggling, still visiting a social worker for counselling about my mental state. But within a matter of weeks, once I had begun to take a conscious interest in spiritual matters and practise daily meditation and prayer at home, opening my heart to the Light and whatever it was to bring, waiting to see my way forward, I received clear instructions. I was shown the task that lay before me and I was shown the assistance I would be given to help me carry it out.

My particular role as a psychic is a relatively simple one. Though I can in fact look into the future and make predictions, that is not what it is all about. After years of wondering how I was best intended to use my powers, even how to describe myself—as a medium, clairvoyant, psychic counsellor, card reader, or all the lot?—I have come to the conclusion that my function is that of a 'wise woman' who is just required to be there when she is needed.

In folk myth this homely person, in cloak and hood, is generally encountered standing at the crossroads. She does not perform magical feats or cast spells, solve problems or give advice. She simply points out to the confused and bewildered traveller the choices he can make, the ways he can choose to go.

I have found that the people who are impelled to consult me quite often do so in crisis situations and need immediate help. Consequently, I rarely take bookings for days or weeks in advance and try to make myself available at any time, whenever the phone rings, rather than carrying out consultations during 'office hours'—unless of course I am working in an established venue with other people.

My function is to clarify and make sense of apparently insoluble problems, to remove the drama from dangerously volatile situations and to throw light into threateningly dark mental and emotional corners. The remark that people most often make to me after a consultation is that 'I had never thought of it that way before.' And yet the choices are always there, for all of us, though the time has to be right for us to see them. Perhaps as the wise woman at the crossroads, what I most often do for people is to help them to 'see clear' for themselves, but not in the way of clairvoyance, which is defined as being able to see things that are not necessarily there. What I do is help people to see what has always been there, what has been there all along, whether perceived or not.

Psychic work is spiritual rather than physical, though it reflects itself in all aspects of physical and material existence. The visions and instructions I received in the weeks after I had begun to attend the Spiritualist Church came during my daily meditation sessions as I sat quietly alone in my flat. My new life of adventure was within my own mind, my journeys were mental ones yet they carried

11

such a sense of truth that I could not doubt their significance and reality, nor the increasing wisdom and enlightenment they brought to me.

Though the psychic and spiritual gifts are given, they have to be worked for and the work that has to be done involves tremendous mental discipline and control. It also necessitates the letting go of one's ego, the 'wanting' side of one's personality, and being willing to place oneself in complete trust and faith in the hands of a greater power—whether one actually perceives that power as God, the Light, the Great Spirit or any other of the names by which it is referred to.

This is a continual process that never ends. It is the whole spiritual journey of life, in the course of which many other spiritual journeys may be made. I found myself travelling into new and unfamiliar realms during those early days as I prayed for guidance and to be shown my way forward.

I thought at the time that what I was given were some kind of basic, preparatory revelations, simple things in images that were all I could take just then, at the 'beginning' as it were, of my psychic existence. But I was to discover as the years progressed and my spiritual wisdom increased, that there is never any 'beginning' to the consciousness of truth, no progression in learning to be wise as we imagine it, in chronological time. The ability to relate to truth—on whatever level this is achieved at any given time—has nothing to do with age, it is a state of mind. And so these images of mine have always remained just as relevant as they were when I first became aware of them, though my understanding has I hope progressed.

The first journeys I made were to a sort of resting place where I was welcomed, comforted, strengthened and reassured of my identity as a 'wise woman'—though this last was in embryonic state then. Two small spirits (I call them that for want of a better word), who were nothing more than tiny embodiments of love and encouragement, made themselves known to me at a very early stage.

I had heard of Spirit Guides at the Spiritualist Church and been told that we all have them—presences to help us on our way through life—but that we have to earn the right to become aware of them and get to know them. I was not quite sure whether I accepted this or not for particularly in the 1920s and 1930s, 'Spirit Guides' became such a cliché outside of spiritual circles that they have been treated ever since to the same kind of irreverence as mothers-in-law in the jokes of stand-up comedians.

One medium at the Church told me that I had a White (or was it Black?) Nun standing at

13

my shoulder who was my Spirit Guide but I found the prospect more embarrassing than inspiring and whoever she was, she never showed up again. I have since learned that we are all given guidance according to our needs.

Some psychics are more at ease when they are working formally with large numbers of Spirit Guides, Gatekeepers, Doorkeepers and other spiritual beings who make communication with other worlds more effective and less hazardous for the living. There are celebrated cases of well loved individual Guides who have been Native American Indians, Chinese Mandarins, saints, monks, nuns, even famous people of the past including surgeons and doctors who can, it is claimed, perform what is known as 'psychic surgery' through the mediums with whom they operate. The native people of America, the ancient Chinese, as well as monks, nuns and so on, were often highly spiritually advanced, which might explain why they seem to appear so much.

But our own Spirit Guides are always personal to us, acceptable and dear in forms we can relate to, whether a famous person, a mystical teacher, a relative or someone we might have known when alive, even an animal or bird. Any kind of spiritual teacher or guardian is always presented to us in such a way that though it might be unexpected, it seems exactly right.

Though I did not feel particularly keen on the idea of the Nun (whether White or Black), I did try to open my mind to accept whatever guidance I might be given and in due course, a figure made its appearance in my meditations. Mysteriously, however, it was under the cover of a long blue velvet cloak and seemed always to be moving ahead of me through a forest of tall trees, the face hidden from me.

I took it to be a woman—and was intrigued to realise that I had actually been aware of 'the woman in the blue cloak' as far back as fifteen years or so previously, when I had seen her in a dream. I had been so struck by the image that I had used it symbolically in one of the novels I had written about a young Victorian musician, *Sing No Sad Songs*.

And now within a few weeks of my new-found state of spiritual awareness I was seeing her again, always moving ahead of me through the tall trunks of the pines, hooded and anonymous. After a while I asked whether she would grant me the privilege of allowing me to see her face. And to my staggered astonishment, the blue cloak collapsed in on itself. Far from the beautiful (or even ugly) woman, nun, Native American Indian, Chinese or any other traditional type of 'Spirit Guide' I had half-anticipated, there was no body there at all. But I found myself looking into the most exquisite little triangular silver face with enormous, expressive silver eyes.

Apart from its face this tiny entity had no form at all, other than being composed of a sort of silvery mist. I concluded later that even the face had been created purely for my benefit, since it allowed me to identify with a spirit which would have been far too difficult for me to envisage—at that stage—as completely disembodied.

I was enchanted with that lovely little face. But the presence of the tiny spirit was not all. I seemed to have been conducted mentally out of the forest of tall trees to a glade that was composed entirely of silver and blue light. There was a kind of small copse where bushes of what I assumed to be flowers were growing in profusion. Later I discovered that the 'flowers' were in fact tiny stars made from the same silver and blue light.

I have no idea even now where this place is, on whatever level of existence. I call it the 'Star Plane' and it is always there when I need to return to it to rest or refresh myself spiritually. It is immensely healing and I have often used the 'star flowers' to assist when I an giving healing to others, as well as mentally gathering armfuls to hold myself if I need to be strengthened before going out to face the world.

As I continued to visit the place in my meditations I discovered another feature apart from the blossoming stars—a 'star-fall' or waterfall but of stars rather than water. Before

I had been guided there I had been practising visualisation, imagining myself standing beneath a real waterfall both for the power this element bestows and for the symbolic cleansing of my spirit and purging of negativity. I found that in this beautiful place I was cleansed and purified beneath a 'fall' of tiny blue stars. There was even a small pool where instead of pebbles, little stars lay waiting to be picked up.

The face of my little spirit continued to enchant me with its loveliness and its unspoken communications of reassurance and love but there was a further surprise to come. My 'guide' had, of course, turned out to be neither male nor female—and one day, stalking through a copse of star-flowers came a second small creature which was even more unconventional. I took it at first to be a cat. However it was not an ordinary cat but in keeping with everything else, a kind of star-cat. Its face was exactly the same as the other, a tiny silver triangle with great silver eyes.

This spirit too was disembodied, though every time it appeared it did provide itself with legs. But the effort of creating a shape for itself (again purely for my benefit), rather than simply appearing like the Cheshire Cat in *Alice in Wonderland* as just a 'grin', did occasionally cause confusion. The little creature often seemed to forget—or not bother about—how many legs it was supposed to have and

17

sometimes possessed five, three or even seven. Being able to 'shape-shift' could be extremely useful though. It reassured me on one occasion when I was dreading a meeting with someone I feared, that I was not to worry because: 'I can give myself a few more mouths if we need them and ten rows of teeth going in all at once would make quite a satisfactory dent in his ankle!'

With recollections of Spirit Guides called by names like 'Grey Owl', 'Ching Li' or 'Hawkwind' I asked these two unexpected little creatures what I should call them. They seemed amused by the request. Names, while important in magic, are spiritually only vibrations on the ether to which the spirit can tune in like a radio signal. They are as unnecessary on more elevated planes as physical bodies.

A few highly sentimental names came into my mind—but they were my own ideas, nothing to do with the reality of the situation. Should I call them Silver Blossom? Blue Moon? (suggested by the lovely star-flowers and the colours of the place). They scoffed at such sentimentality. The first agreed to be called 'Blue' if it had to have a name, while the star-cat was of the opinion that the most realistic and useful part of a flower was its stalk. So 'Blue and Stalk' like some sort of cosmic double-act, they have always been, though I generally think of them as just 'the

18

Little Spirits'.

'Blue' is immensely gentle and loving and over the years has given me great comfort when I most needed it. 'Stalk' is tough and laid-back with an acid tongue. When it is straight talk that has been needed, a shaking of myself out of complacency or smugness, a bursting of the bubbles of arrogance, pride or self-pity, then 'Stalk' provides it.

Much later when I was ready to accept it, I learned that the true source of my spiritual guidance was far greater and deeper than had at first appeared. 'Blue' and 'Stalk' were only sparks, as it were, of the real fire. I do not have a 'Spirit Guide' as such, in some familiar form with a name. I know it only as 'Mist', the name I gave it when I became aware of its existence in its natural state, resembling nothing else but a swirling core of silver mist, pure energy. It is from this source that my enlightenment and answers, the teachings and truths I live by and include in my work and writing, are drawn.

CHAPTER TWO

THE WAY FORWARD

There is no need for anyone in this life ever to feel helpless or alone for we are surrounded by all kinds of unseen beings, spirits, angels and carers whose only desire is to assist us along our spiritual path. Advice, guidance, wisdom, truth and all the information we need about everything—including practical assistance to enable us to cope in the physical, material world—is available if only we are willing to open our ears, eyes and minds to it.

The number of people who regularly 'speak' to their departed mother, father, grandad or other relative would amaze cynics who think they know better than to believe the soul lives on after death. Conversations are being conducted all the time with the dead and in most cases spontaneously, without the help of a medium, though some people feel better if they follow the traditional rituals of consulting someone who, they consider, is better equipped to venture into the world of the departed to deliver their messages and bring back the advice or information they request.

Most cultures recognise the importance of considering our ancestors, of appreciating the ways in which those who have gone before can help, inspire and guide those who are struggling with living in the present. In some cases this can be regarded as a tribal or communal thing—when we consider the example of saints or great leaders of the past for instance, for their influence is more general and can benefit everyone. But equally valid is the continuing presence, often, of our own dear ones, ordinary people maybe who lived quietly and unspectacularly and never hit the headlines or achieved recognition outside the family circle. In cases of need such spirits will just as lovingly help and advise those who looked to them for comfort and guidance when they were on the earth, even if they are no longer present in the flesh.

Psychic or spiritual awareness brings home more than anything else the fact that, as John Donne so famously phrased it, 'No man is an island.' Whether we like it or not we are all connected, not by our achievements or our piety or worth but by the simple fact of our existence. In the simplistic but lovely images of Buddhism every living thing possesses a spark of the 'Buddha nature', just as according to the beliefs of Christianity every one of God's creatures enshrines a tiny fragment of God himself. And it is this spark, this divine drop of pure gold, which links us all.

Psychics are most often consulted when individuals need to make some kind of decision. Well-balanced people who feel confident in their own judgements seldom bother to have their cards read or to question what previous existences they might have experienced; it is the anxious souls, concerned about making the correct choice or proceeding along 'the right way', who come to ask for guidance or advice.

In fact there is no one 'right way' in life. There are many ways and whichever one chooses, one will eventually arrive at the end of the journey. What is important is to have commitment to the way one has chosen and to take responsibility for the decisions one has made and will make. Everyone is intuitively aware of the appropriate way for them to go, the way that is at that moment right for them whether it is conventionally morally 'good' or socially 'right' or not. Sometimes the best and most appropriate way is actually the easiest but early conditioning in life and a lack of self-worth can lay a terrible burden of guilt on the prospect of a future with no sacrifice or struggling. This is why so many people cling blindly to a way of living that is difficult or even painful when they could quite easily smooth out their path—as I have discussed in the chapter on 'Coming to Terms'.

Advice is always available, however, if we do not feel competent to make decisions for ourselves and there are signposts along the road of life to point out the next stage of every journey. One of the things which stands in the way of making a choice is the part of our personality I mentioned earlier—the ego, the 'wanting' side that finds it impossible to just stand back dispassionately and weigh up the pros and cons. The clamouring voice of the ego is so loud that we are unable to hear the 'still small voice' that is always ready to give us spiritual guidance—from whatever source this comes—if we genuinely seek it.

At the beginning of my psychic career I felt very much in need of spiritual help. All the people I met who seemed to know their way round in this world that was unfamiliar to me, both at the Spiritualist Church and elsewhere, gave me different counsel based on their own opinions. Which was 'right', I too wondered in confusion; which was the best way—or the best for me?

I placed my faith in God, in my prayers and meditations and the hours I spent alone in my flat waiting for guidance from that higher power. And the second series of mental journeys I made in those early days took me to a very different place to the 'Star Plane'. At first I could not understand why I was being shown it nor its significance to me. It came in glimpses which, as with all spiritual awareness, intensified in detail as I progressed.

When I mentioned it to all those other people more experienced in such matters,

23

assuming they had made the same mental journey and would be able to tell me more about the place I had seen, I found none of them was able to do so. But they reacted to my accounts with great unease. One leading member of the Spiritualist Church even ordered me solemnly to stop all psychic activity because I was obviously on very dangerous ground. Yet though I found the place filled with pain and anguish I never felt frightened nor afraid to be there, nor in any danger myself though I had experienced the threat of spiritual danger on previous occasions in my life.

What I saw there first was a tall, cowled figure standing at the bottom of what seemed to be a sheer cliff. Over the cliff poured what I thought at first was a waterfall. (Waterfalls seem to mean a great deal to me and in life, too, I find them very meaningful and significant. Water represents strength and power and I love it although I am afraid of deep water, and cannot swim.)

When the scene clarified itself a little I realised that every single thing in it including the air, ground, cliff and whatever was pouring down over it—even the sky and whatever illuminated the place—was the same colour. It is a colour I have never seen on Earth and never want to see. A sort of reddish-brown that seems to be made up of the colours of both wet and dried blood, entrails, excrement, burning dust, burning rock, parched clay, ashes—impossible to describe. A terrifying colour that gives the impression that this is a lost place, a place where no visitors come, where nothing grows, where all hope has been abandoned.

During my early visits I spoke to the cowled figure asking for enlightenment. His robe, though dark, was different to everything else in the place and I never saw his face nor felt the need to see it. But I did ask his name. He said he was the Gatekeeper, which did not mean anything to me at the time though I discovered later that Gatekeepers are beings which guard the entrances and exits from other realms and which many psychic travellers apparently encounter quite often. I have to admit, though, that I have never yet met another one.

The Gatekeeper seemed to possess some object he wanted to pass on to me. It appeared to be some kind of stone, a sort of fiery red, burning coal. I took it into my hands but when I asked what it was, the only answer I received was, 'Provisions'. I did not understand but assumed that I was about to go on some sort of journey and that this object would fortify me along the way, though I had no idea how.

I still do not know what this object was, though I have since encountered various similar descriptions of a bestowing of spiritual power in different cultures. The burning cloud, the fiery stone or coal appears to symbolise the burning away of darkness, negativity and evil and the force by which this may be achieved. The fiery coal placed into my hands was, I think now, the power to undertake the task I was about to be shown.

Again and again I found myself returning to the familiar, dreadful landscape, compelled to keep going back even though, as I have said, people whose advice I asked all told me: 'Keep away. It doesn't sound the sort of place you want to go.' But I felt within me that I was being taken there for a purpose, even though I did not yet know what the purpose was.

Eventually, when I asked the Gatekeeper whether he could reveal more to me he was ready. He turned my gaze from the cliff and the waterfall which was all I had so far seen of the place, and I found I was looking out across a flat plateau that seemed to extend into infinity.

It was a ghastly sight. There were no trees, no landmarks, no sign of anything except the surface of the plateau itself which seemed to be deep with clinging mud of the same horrible colour as the rest of the place. In the mud, wallowing and struggling, figures were lying. They were piled up, lifting themselves desperately onto their elbows, sliding back again, raising blinded eyes filled with mud and trying to call for assistance through the mud that clogged their mouths. There were hundreds of them—thousands. The whole

26

scene was one seething mass of despair.

I seemed to see dim shapes of cannon lodged in the mud and the fallen bodies of horses. I realised though that my impressions of the Crimea, or some other unidentifiable war, were only there to prompt me to the fact that I was looking at the aftermath of a gigantic battle. I assumed that these were the wounded, left behind, and that they needed help.

It is important to record that though I was aware of the suffering and the pain, though I seemed to feel the agonies of every soul myself, I was at the same time utterly detached from it all. This detachment is something that must be learned—and constantly worked at to maintain—before anyone can function effectively as a psychic or indeed in any other respect if one wishes to be of assistance to other people. Particularly in psychic and spiritual matters it is possible to feel and experience (to 'pick up') the weight and darkness that may surround other people, and be tempted sometimes to carry their negativity or try to go down their fated path for them. But in the end that does not help either them or you.

A psychic, a healer—anyone of wisdom— learns to empathise intensely with others and yet remain aloof from their tragedies. He must be prepared to offer assistance or guidance, but respect the absolute right of others to choose whether they will accept it or not.

The Gatekeeper told me that I was looking at the mission that had been assigned to me. It was among the figures struggling on this awful plain of red mud that my task lay. For a wild moment I had a vision of myself in some sort of Red Cross armband, stepping into the mud with a willingness to assist but no resources, only my empty hands to try and help this monumental suffering, ease this unbearable pain.

I could not at first believe what I was being told, or take it in. I was not equipped even to contemplate trying to tackle the sort of task that seemed to lie in front of me. I was relatively inexperienced I felt, a comparative beginner along the path that had so recently been revealed to me. This was surely a task for an expert, for someone whose powers were proved, of formidable strength. Had I got that sort of strength and power? Yet if this was the way I was to go I had to accept it, whatever it involved.

I had heard mention of Spirit Rescue Circles where 'lost' or trapped spirits were assisted by workers of wide experience to find their way home to the Light. I wondered whether this was what the vision signified. Was I to become a member of a Spirit Rescue Circle?

Over the period of time while I absorbed

28

and tried to make sense of what I had been told I did actually try to join several Psychic Circles in various parts of London, again hoping that more experienced people would advise me. I soon realised, however, that I was being given clear indications from the spirit world that working in such groups was not—at least, at that time—for me.

I seemed to have been marked out to work alone though I had no real idea of how I was to go about it. But there was no sign of anyone else on that awful plain, no sign that anyone else would ever come there. Even the fact that everyone had warned me to keep away and avoid my visions of the place of suffering, seemed to indicate that it was not somewhere where most people—even psychics—would willingly go.

Yet I felt intuitively that the Gatekeeper was right. Wherever, whatever this place was it was here that my work lay, and recalling how 'the Little Spirits' had so miraculously appeared, I began to realise that I would be given the strength and power I might need. I did not face my task alone. I would be given help.

There was, however, a problem. The next time I returned I told the Gatekeeper that I was willing to do what I could, to accept my task but—I had no idea of where the plain of red mud was. Certainly it was nowhere I recognised or had ever heard of. It looked like it might be on some other planet. How was I to get there? How was I to find these pitiful lost souls so that I could help them?

His reply was simple. He said:

'They will come to you.'

Within weeks of beginning to attend the Spiritualist Church I had become aware that I possessed psychic and mediumistic powers and also that I was a natural healer. Within months I had been given instructions as to my future work and promised all the help and strength I would need to fulfil my task. Within less than a year, I was working as a professional psychic, travelling all over the South of England.

This sort of thing is the stuff of drama, of fiction. It is such an unbelievable tale that I don't think I would have dared to include it in any novel of mine as the readers would not have believed it could happen. And yet, as I was soon to discover, the unbelievable happens all the time if you let it. I learned to accept miracles as a part of everyday living. The turn my life was taking soon proved to be proof of that.

In case I had not believed the Gatekeeper's words that if I was needed the wounded souls would find me, I literally bumped into the first of them almost immediately—a young man who looked like the cliché Greek god and was charismatically charming with it. I encountered him in a shop in the North End Road that sold New Age objects and gem stones, and felt myself chilled and shaken at the cloud of negativity and darkness I sensed around him.

I had to make a split-second decision. I did not know him, but I could see he was in desperate need of help for all his smiling, easy manner. But I had been instructed, as all aspiring psychics and healers are, not to force help on anyone unless it was asked for—and perhaps, I thought uneasily, just perhaps I was making some awful mistake. Perhaps my awareness of that dark cloud was quite inaccurate, perhaps if I spoke to him I would simply be making a fool of myself. After all, I was just an ordinary passer-by, a middle-aged writer—.

As all these thoughts flashed through my head I knew somehow that this was my first test. I could walk on, say nothing, go home and continue to 'be spiritual' in the privacy of my flat—or I could make a statement of my faith in what Spirit and the Gatekeeper had told me, what I felt within myself to be the real truth. Even if the young man's cry for help was unspoken, I knew it was there. So, hardly able to accept what I was doing, I stopped him outside the shop, said that I was psychic and a healer, that I believed he was in need of help, and asked whether he would like to talk to me. The result was that we sat together on a bench outside a pub and he talked for two hours.

I had really been thrown into the deep end,

as it were. Jon (not his real name) came from a very wealthy, upper-class background but he had lost his job, was on the point of being thrown out of the house he shared with two other people, had run through the fortune he had inherited at twenty-one and was desperate and penniless. And he had been a heroin addict for five years.

I had to make a real commitment of faith in Spirit and in the destiny that had been revealed to me, to consciously let go of all the things that had previously seemed to matter so much in my life—a career, the accumulation of money, a cocoon from unpleasantness, the prospect of fitting myself into a respectable middle-age as life drifted towards the safe security of becoming elderly and enjoying the traditional 'golden years' in retirement—.

Jon said I helped him just by being there, so I did what I felt I reasonably could. An addict lives very much from day to day, even minute to minute, so I went along to his house each afternoon for an hour or so to see him; bought him meals as we sat talking in the café round the corner; tried to give him confidence in himself. Everyone I knew assumed I had simply lost my head over a good-looking younger man; they warned me that I was a fool, I would be taken advantage of, and so on.

My answer was that what was given freely could not be taken advantage of. I did not expect to be rewarded and neither did I realistically expect to make any actual difference. But I chose to be there, to contribute in my way as a sort of pledge of my good faith, my willingness to do my best in the task I had undertaken.

I had no money to give Jon but I gave him my time and talked to him about his situation, his family, his emotional problems—even his girl-friends. We discussed philosophy and spiritual matters. I gave him healing, kept him company. I soon learned a very great deal about a distressing world I had never entered, that of the addict on hard drugs. But Jon took great care never to embarrass me and was touchingly considerate of my feelings. I began to see that by being willing to contribute I was being paid back in lessons of experience that could never have been acquired any other way.

My flat had only one big room but when Jon was thrown out of his house, I allowed him to camp out for a week on my living-room floor while other accommodation was found, though by this time I was being solemnly warned by everyone I knew that it was only a matter of time before I realised the increasing error of my ways. 'Heroin addicts are beyond help,' I was informed, 'they are incurable, he just wants money for his fix. You'll be robbed.'

But Jon never robbed me—of anything. And though I had not seriously hoped for this outcome—or indeed had any expectations at all, accepting Jon as he was—it remains a fact that he made the decision to come off drugs and was able to free himself from methadone, the heroin substitute, and drastically reduce all the other drugs he took, including Valium, within eight months. He achieved this 'cold turkey' on his own in a bed-sit in Earl's Court and in due course, after he was 'clean', he went to try and sort himself out to begin a new life in the country he felt was his spiritual home—India. He had previously given me a postcard on which he had written: 'To the first real lady I have ever met. Thank you for saving my soul'.

There were other people who loved Jon and who helped him more than I was able to do. But perhaps my intervention outside the New Age shop provided something in the nature of a catalyst for his eventual recovery; perhaps, like the hooded figure at the crossroads, I had to just 'be there' to point out a way he had never been able to see clearly before.

This was my first, possibly the most traumatic 'case' of my psychic career and it taught me, possibly, even more than it taught Jon. It taught me never to be judgmental, to have hope even in the most terrible of circumstances, that 'being there' can be more important than all the money in the world. It taught me that faith, love and trust can indeed perform miracles against all the odds. And it taught me that it is never too late for anything, never too late to begin again—or just to begin.

My life took yet another turn. At the Spiritualist Church I met Richard, an astrologer and clairvoyant who seemed to recognise the powers I was as yet so unsure of. It seemed as though we had been fated to meet and because he talked 'my' language and we seemed to have been meant to be and work together, I found a whole new way of existence opening up for me.

I had prayed for guidance as to how I would manage if, in my spiritual progress, it was necessary to sacrifice my small securities and luxuries—even the little day to day income I lived on—and the reassuring reply had come:

'Enough will be provided for your needs.'

In fact, this promise has been kept ever since. The Spirit does provide enough—just. Sometimes it comes from the strangest sources, and most unexpectedly. But on the spiritual path, what is needed is always found somehow, though one is generally given no more than basic essentials. I was shown how I might be able to manage spiritually in a material society, a way of working to earn my living.

As soon as I met Richard I found myself introduced to the world of Psychic Fairs and psychics in general. I had never, as I have mentioned, ever encountered psychics *en masse*—just visited that local lady who read my cards—and I had hardly heard of Psychic Fairs.

But after accompanying Richard to one or two as a spectator I was invited to take part in a large fair at Torquay with him—in my own right—and we set off to the coast in his almost vintage Hillman Avenger, hoping we would make it safely for our working weekend by the sea.

Psychic Fairs are gatherings of mediums, psychics, clairvoyants, Tarot readers, people who sell crystals and gem stones, New Age music, North American Indian artifacts, numerologists, palmists, astrologers—anything and everything connected with the world of the psychic and the occult, which the public is invited to visit and patronise. You can get your problems sorted out, find your own inner beauty and tranquillity, buy a gem stone, have a cup of tea and spend time drinking in food for the soul as well as the beverage in your cup.

Most Psychic Fairs have a wonderfully uplifting atmosphere—though as I was to discover later when I came to know many of the psychics who 'worked the circuits' in the South of England, some of them are as difficult to cope with as operatic prima donnas and will throw fits of temperament at the drop of a Tarot card. There can be clashes of ego and a good deal of personal aggrandisement. This happens in spiritual circles just as much as anywhere else. Indeed, it appears that someone who has been given psychic gifts often feels a need to fight for his or her place and survival—perhaps because in the historic past, many such people were literally persecuted simply because they possessed the gifts of 'seeing' and healing.

The fair at Torquay was scheduled for Sunday and Bank Holiday Monday at the end of August. I was confident I would be able to cope, largely because Richard had confidence in me and I had unlimited confidence in his judgement over such matters. But on the evening before we set out, there was a milestone to be passed. I had not felt my name as a writer was right for a psychic, and had hastily ordered some of the small handbills (generally referred to as 'leaflets') which psychics use to advertise themselves and explain the type of work they do.

Late on Friday evening, these were delivered. I had chosen what I considered a more suitable name rather erratically from one of my own books and here it was before me, looking very impressive and professional. Dilys Gater the novelist and writer had become:

DAWN ROSE
Clairvoyant and Psychic Medium

As it happened, there was no need for me to worry about how I would manage as a professional psychic. The powers are always there and once you have learned to be conscious of them, you draw on the same powers which will be accessible to you many years later. All that changes is your own experience and awareness. The truth remains the same.

The scene I recall most vividly from that weekend—which was perhaps the strangest, most unexpected and unusual weekend in my life—was one which seemed to give me, as I stood at my own particular crossroads, a message that all was well. There was nothing to fear even though I had turned my back, as it were, on my past with its familiarity and security and was stepping into a world of demons and dragons where my feet might sink at any moment into those quaking sands of red mud, and even if I reached out, there might be nothing to hold onto.

On Monday morning we rose early at the cottage where we had stayed, packed our bags and drove into Torquay before the Fair was open. Richard parked his car on the side of a hill near some railings, where there was a view down over a railway cutting and across the sea far below. It was cold, with a hint of autumn in the air, and the world seemed very quiet. Early mist was still tangled across the grass and shrubs beyond the railings.

Richard walked some way off and I was alone with just the mist and the sunrise, the seas amaranthine below, a few wild flowers within reach of my hand, lovely insignificant blossoms that by the coming of twilight would have lived their brief lives. I took a few flowers and leaves, giving thanks to the Earth with a welling up of almost unbearable emotion within my heart.

The feeling of communication between myself and the Earth and the Spirit which had guided me to that moment safely and shown me the way I was to go, was as fragile as a drop of dew or the iridescence of a dragonfly's wing, as intense and as lovely. I had given nothing up that mattered—and I had been blessed with everything that most wonderfully mattered, which I had long since given up all hope of achieving.

I stayed a few moments quietly on my own, then went to Richard and gave him the flowers. Then we went on to the Fair.

CHAPTER THREE

TAKE A MESSAGE

Drenched with sunlight in the landscape of 12th Century England, an old monk sits in his garden where the scents of herbs, bitter and pungent, rise like incense on the golden air. He nods, half-asleep, the abbey walls dreaming darkly behind him.

In mediaeval times the sons of noble families were sent to be educated in such abbeys by the monks, and we can picture them sitting or sprawling in their vivid doublets on summer afternoons in the shade of the cloisters. Eager to pursue their hawking and their hunting, they would have listened to an old man's simple advice on how to live a good life with the same restlessness as the young Romeo listened to Friar Lawrence discourse on the medicinal properties of plants in *Romeo and Juliet.*

'A good life, my children, what is that? Is it good to sit with hands raised to heaven in saintliness while a beggar crawls unheeded at your feet? Is it good to lift a child from the mud and place its feet on a firm path, or to sit and discourse learnedly with it on the theories of Jerome and Crassus?

'What is goodness but a reflection of the face of God, a glimpse of what is visible to the angels and to which they sing their praises in constancy—for this is necessary, for can the wonders ever be counted? Yet in this life we are not yet angels, my children, we have not the voices to sing and so we must chirp like small birds our thankfulness and praise. We cannot yet sing the great intricate harmonies of the angels, but a small sound and even such as has no sound at all.

'For goodness is the echo of angelic singing in this life, a glimpse only and a soft note that others as well as God may hear. Falling water and the silence of the rock is such a song, for the best goodness is for each to be truly itself in joy and love; and so if we are ourselves and assist others to be themselves also, this is the song that will sound most sweet as it rises to the throne of God . . .'

These words and many others from different sources are transcripts I have made over the years of texts that have been 'channelled' or dictated spiritually to me. As a medium I am often required to contact spirits in the world of the dead and pass messages to or from the living—or the other way about. These are generally of a personal nature but the messages that come to psychics who receive 'channelled' material are usually far wider in their scope. They are gifts from the spiritual

41

world to everyone who seeks hope and encouragement, enlightenment and inspiration to help them on their way. Many such texts have been published in their own right and are recognised classics of spiritual teaching, their sources fully acknowledged.

I first became aware of the presence of the old monk and the image of his garden in 1997 in the unexpected setting of a coffee shop in the King's Road in London. While drinking my coffee and waiting for a friend I felt impelled to scribble down some sentences that seemed to be in the process of dictation within my head, though I did not know where they were coming from. It was only after several days, by which time the text extended to more pages, that my mental image clarified itself and I discovered I had made contact with Brother Gregory, an Augustinian monk who had lived in the late 1100s somewhere in the South of England.

The messages contained in the words were simple and unassuming, the result of Brother Gregory's lifetime of prayer and contemplation within the confines of his abbey. The inspiration for his imagery was his love of God and his love of the natural world, particularly his own small plot of garden. I was rather surprised to find myself in touch with him but his words were extremely appropriate since at first I thought they were intended for an old friend I had known when I had lived in the Midlands, who had in 1997 suddenly reappeared in my life. Paul, like Brother Gregory, was also a gardener—a horticulturist—who was going through a very difficult time just then.

As I wrote the early messages down I passed them on to Paul. But later it became obvious that the good brother's words were far more inspiring than I had originally thought. Some were directed at the specific needs of a wider public—'a lonely woman' or 'one who has suffered the loss of joy', for instance.

Gifts from the spiritual world can take the most unexpected forms. It seemed at one point as though the original mediaeval monk's garden itself was being 'given' to us as well as his wise and encouraging words. I was interested enough to try to describe what I had seen of the garden and to make notes on the herbs and flowers growing there. Paul, whose work involves the designing and creation of gardens, became so personally involved with my project that he felt prompted to research and draw up a plan he thought of creating and planting himself.

We even began to work on a book to be called *Brother Gregory's Garden*. This as yet unfinished volume was intended to reflect the tranquillity of that sunny little mediaeval plot with its fragrances bitter and sweet, its subtle shades of petal and leaf. Coloured plates and descriptions of the plants and herbs that would have grown in a mediaeval monk's garden, notes on their various uses and properties as medicines and in the still-room, all to be accompanied by extracts from Brother Gregory's teachings—one day perhaps, it will be completed.

But in a way there is no need for Brother Gregory's garden lives through his words. Serene and simple, spiritually wise yet with a deep sense of humanity, his unquestioning faith in God's bounty and the abundance of life and its gifts shines from every line and continues to be an inspiration. I could gain no more information about his abbey than that it was somewhere in the South of England, and no more about the man himself than that he lived in the half-century after the Battle of Hastings, but it is as though I know him well.

Some of his words are included in Chapter Eight of this book and everyone who reads and appreciates them will, I am sure, feel as I do that they have been granted a great privilege. They have been able to sit with those young noblemen, his students and scholars, sharing the experience of listening to an old man steeped in holiness yet understanding of human failings, pass on his teaching and his blessing in that long-gone abbey garden in the sunlight and scent of a summer afternoon.

It was very early on in my psychic career that I first began to receive 'channelled' messages

44

from spiritual sources. Having worked throughout my adult life in the writing profession—first as a journalist and later as a novelist and the author of non-fiction books (including three giving advice on how to write)—words have always been my trade and I am familiar with the getting of ideas and 'inspiration'. I had always felt previously that they were my own, personal to my way of thinking and writing even though they often seemed to spring from my subconscious and surprise me. This process happens with every creative person—any other writer will tell you the same thing.

But once I began to realise I was mediumistic and had gained some experience of consciously communicating with the dead, passing messages between the worlds of spiritual and physical, I seemed to be intuitively able to open up my mind so that I could transcribe quite long and detailed texts which came from sources 'outside' rather than 'inside' myself. As they began to arrive I wrote them down, either in longhand or straight onto my word processor, and kept them stored in folders and binders.

Many people are able to 'channel' in this way though not all of them are psychic. Many psychics, in fact, do not conduct two-way communication with spirits at all, whether they are the spirits of the dead or any other kind. And many mediums who are able to pass on messages from departed souls do not make any claim to be psychic or 'second sighted'. The actual nature of the psychic gift—whether this also involves mediumistic ability or not—can be very difficult to define.

In my own case, for instance, it took me years before I realised that the most convenient way of describing my own psychic ability was to call it 'second sight'. I am clairvoyant. I can 'read' the Tarot cards, playing cards, people's palms or whatever else I may be required to use as a focus for 'second sight' equally effectively. I can pass messages to and from the world of the dead, and much else besides. Generally I suppose I am what you might call an 'all-rounder' though this was not because I consciously had any choice in the matter. I found out what my capabilities were as my experience increased and I was confronted with problems and situations that took me into new, unfamiliar areas of psychic work. The same principles apply to spiritual growth and maturity as to our physical growth—it is an ongoing thing and the learning process never stops, however apparently advanced one might be.

As a writer myself I had tried various methods of automatic writing out of interest before I became aware of my psychic potential, but the results had been just a scribble. In fact I did not really believe, even when I had started my psychic career, that it was possible for an outside entity to 'write' anything with another person's hand. I did not see how this would work—particularly, I did not see how it could be done on a computer or any other type of machine.

What I had not realised was that I had been thinking in *purely physical* terms, assuming the physical brain would control the hand as it had done in my own previous writing. Even in poetry or the most apparently 'inspired' type of composition the brain is always to some extent in control. But once I learned to concentrate on allowing what was being communicated to just filter through *mentally*— using my brain and hand as a kind of automatic pick-up or receiver and adding nothing myself—I found I was able to 'channel' very easily.

The first time it happened consciously was in those amazing few months after I had met Richard and begun my career as a psychic. I had been trying to find some suitable material for a short series of inspirational booklets I had put together, intended to be carried in pocket or handbag and to encourage meditation rather than inform. Richard had written one on the *Wisdom of the Tarot* but I did not feel my own psychic experience or spiritual wisdom was developed enough to be offered in book form. A deadline for copy was fast approaching, however, and the two other

47

booklets that had been planned (one by a lady who claimed a past life in the ancient kingdom of Lemuria and another by a young woman who seemed to be in touch with earth spirits) had not materialised.

So one day I sat down at my word processor with the vague idea that I must write something, even though I did not know what I wanted to say. I asked the spirits for guidance and then, deliberately not looking at the screen, I tapped out whatever letters the incoming images and impulses prompted, letting all just flow through my mind and making no effort to interpret or make sense of it.

When I felt too tired to concentrate any longer I had a look at the result of my experiment and was amazed and thrilled. The words that had come up on the screen were some of the most beautiful I had ever read, and I knew with absolute certainty that the mind which had 'dictated' them had not been my own.

'In the texture of the water are my footprints and in the green leaves is my touch; I walk on the wings of the morning and the silk robe of the night showers me with stars.

'For the maiden is the crown of the mysteries, studded with round stones that are my gems; from the sacred chalice springs the wine of ecstasy, and across the great arch of the sky the

starry bodies meet in passionate joy.'

Further material was to be forthcoming when, in great excitement, I continued the experiment the following day and during the days that followed.

'I am the Goddess of the silver spring who led the unicorn by a thread of crimson safely through the tangled thickets of the forest, and before whom the giant babe-eater, Behemoth—foaming blood as he gnashed his teeth and screamed his misery to the stars, hiding their sacred fires—knelt to kiss the tip of my robe. Prostrate he lay and from the black hole of his mouth streamed the black slime of the knowledge of evil; and upon the surface of the water near alighted a white swan, to fade like a wraith of loveliness into the dusk, and the night darkened . . .

'Prepare the altar and light the flame for I am come. Though there be no gatherers in my name, yet still from the glaciers of the north and the waterfalls of the south I will come, though the time be long and the waiting wearisome. Though there is no shadow to greet me, yet I am come, and because of my presence the small creatures in the forest relax their vigilance and sleep, and the hunted deer rests her weariness, and the trapped resign their souls and die . . .'

I was given more than enough material for the next of our inspirational booklets, which appeared under the title *Wisdom of the Goddess*. Though I had only the vaguest idea who 'the Goddess' was, I could not help being fascinated by the strength as well as the beauty of the 'Goddess texts' with their powerful imagery. They seemed to reflect a more truthful interpretation of life than many 'sweetness and light' teachings I had previously encountered which had not helped me personally during the difficult periods of my own life. But these words that had been given, as it were, directly to me and to the needs of my new existence, steadied me and gave me steadfastness and courage.

I found in them that the seeming harshness—often cruelty—of natural existence was faithfully mirrored with no self-pitying sentimentality. The inevitability of death and sacrifice occurred even in the most beautiful passages and suffering was not minimised. Yet there was comfort here too, for suffering and pain was placed into a wider context alongside such wonderful images as the complete redeeming power of unconditional love and the sense of an impersonal as well as a personal destiny.

I have included some of the 'Goddess texts', together with background information on their source, in Chapter Eight of this book. The Goddess and Brother Gregory offer counsel, inspiration and advice for living from two very different viewpoints—and yet as with all truly

50

enlightened spiritual teaching, their messages are, in essence, exactly the same.

It is not easy to explain to those who have no experience of such things how psychics receive communications from disembodied or discarnate spirits, or any other sources outside themselves. Someone who possesses the gift of clairaudience (which means 'hearing clear' or 'hearing true') may actually 'hear voices' in a physical sense though the speakers are not physically present. Most of the psychics I have encountered do not claim to possess this ability, and I do not possess it myself or, at least, only to a limited degree. I cannot answer for other psychics, but the messages and information I receive from other realms (whether 'channelled' or as a result of contact with a spirit, ghost or whatever else) are nearly always in the form of a kind of coded signal—something like Braille or Morse—which has to be interpreted into words before being passed on.

Sometimes the message is a simple one which can be 'translated' into just one sentence, but often huge amounts of information involving potentials, possibilities and other intangibles are communicated in what seems like a fraction of a second. The complexities of such a process can be compared to the complexities of a mathematical formula—and in fact though most people are unaware of it, there are very great similarities between the principles of mathematics and physics and the principles of the psychic world.

Whether the information I receive is obtained by means of ESP (Extra Sensory Perception), telepathy, 'second sight' or anything else, I cannot tell you. All I know is that it comes.

As 'channelled' material passes through my mind there is no sense of lettering or punctuation, only the meaning itself. When I write the words down I add only what is necessary in the form of full stops, commas and capital letters to break up the continuous flow into sentences and make these coherent to a reader. As with all such messages from the spirit or other realms, though, the psychic is bound to pass these on *exactly* as they are given so I never alter the meanings or the words themselves, even if they do not make sense to me at the time. Often I have not understood the messages at first, or felt they were odd or obscure, but their deeper meaning or symbolism has emerged later.

In the case of Brother Gregory I found instances where some tiny detail had to be expressed so exactly that I had to struggle with it to get it exactly as the old monk wanted it. The following paragraph, for instance, was one such case. It was in a context using the imagery describing the spiritual quest of a knight of mediaeval times and I originally wrote it down as follows:

'*Within the deepest water and the barest peak where the brown brushwood burned by the summer touches the coppery of the sun and dull gleam of the sky, you will lay down your sword and offer yourself to the Goddess who arches across the universe day to day, morn to evening, and you will find in her the power to transform and transfigure, to initiate you to knighthood in the mysteries.*'

I could not understand the words 'coppery of the sun' and worried over them but did not alter them since I was sure they were accurate. I pondered on them again and again until at last, months later, I realised in a flash of intuitive understanding that the brother had been right and it had been my ability as a 'translator' that was at fault. What he had given me was 'the copper EYE of the sun', but I had, as it were, misheard him, taking 'eye' as 'y'—they do sound almost exactly the same and on this occasion I had to some extent been aware of the sound.

When I began my psychic work and was confused about how to describe myself— whether as a clairvoyant, a medium or whatever—I asked Richard what he thought my function was. He replied (rather obscurely, I considered then): 'You are an interpreter.' I have managed in the years since then to make some of the obscurities of psychic work and theory more available to the general public in my three books, so I hope that means he was right.

But all psychics and mediums are actually interpreters. Psychic ability—particularly 'second sight', which as in my own case can encompass almost everything—is the ability not only to see and be aware of things in the past, present and future which are not visible to our physical senses, but to be open to something much deeper, the hidden truth beyond the superficial. 'Second sight' is not in fact a seeing at all but a kind of knowing, an inner certainty.

The 'seeing' part of psychic work is actually quite basic—it is relatively easy to learn to develop one's innate clairvoyant power so that one can 'see things'. The psychic's knowledge and skill shows itself in what is called the 'interpretation'—being able to grasp and, if necessary, convey accurately to others the true meaning and significance of what is seen. And it is in the pursuit of such truth that a diviner or seer—someone like myself, if they feel they have a vocation or calling—will want to devote his or her whole life.

A medium who passes messages between the spiritual and physical does not actually 'do' anything save act as a way or a means by which communication can be made. Another word like way or path is 'channel', which is what the term 'channelled' material refers to. But whatever the message contains should not— and generally does not, if properly handled— affect the person who is passing it on though sometimes, when dealing with the spirits of the dead, one can pick up emotions or physical sensations as well as mental communication.

It is a little strange at first to find oneself aware of chest pressure and breathing difficulties when communicating with a spirit who died of some asphyxiating illness, or experiencing the sensation of paralysis caused when the communicator had suffered a stroke and was unable to move or speak. Causes of death can also make themselves apparent. I have dealt with many cases where, without being informed of any of the facts by my sitter, I have been aware that the dead person had committed suicide and been able to describe the method that was used. Sometimes it is possible to know that the spirit had suffered a long and debilitating illness or a long period of pain before passing, or that death was sudden and violent, perhaps in a crash.

This awareness does not hurt the medium in any way, and neither do any other manifestations that are revealed through the medium. But they can appear distressing— even frightening—to an onlooker or even to the medium if he or she is not prepared for them and is not advised about what they are and how they should be handled. I have recently dealt with two cases which are relevant in this connection.

The first took place at a Psychic Fair in Buxton. A lady sat down for a session with me and said rather haltingly that she needed some help in 'putting my act together'. The cards showed me that she was recovering from depression, and she revealed that she had been ill for some time so that even now she found it difficult to cope with the stress of everyday living.

As we talked, I began to be aware of physical manifestations in her face, changes which, fortunately, I was able to recognise and identify though I have only rarely encountered them. It was as though, very subtly, the structure of her face altered in the same sort of way one image on a computer can flow into another. Her bone structure appeared to become more pronounced, her skin seemed to darken. The face of the blonde, middle-aged woman became, as I looked into her eyes, that of a bronzed and elderly man and yet—somehow the face was still the same.

The changes were so subtle and seemed to fluctuate so much—and I knew she was not aware of them herself—that it took a little time before I was sure enough to tell her what I was seeing.

'Whatever else you may or may not be, you are a medium, you know, a transfiguration medium. Your Guide is a Native American Indian, he is with you now and I can see him in your face. Most commonly, the medium just passes on messages from his or her Guide, but you will be able to take on his appearance and probably, when you are more used to it, speak in his voice too.'

We had been discussing the spiritual and psychic work she had been doing and she was able to take this though she found it a little disconcerting. I told her that I had met few transfiguration mediums before—and never such a powerfully visual one.

'Have you felt the presence of your Guide?' I asked, and she shook her head.

'Not really—though you are right about the voice. I did have one experience where, when I was just waking up and I wasn't sure whether I was really awake or asleep, I found myself speaking in this deep voice that seemed to come from—I don't know, right deep in my abdomen, saying things I had no control over, strange things. It was—well, disturbing. Weird.'

'What did you feel when it happened?' I asked her. 'You have a most wonderful gift and I think transfiguration mediums are quite rare. But of course, if you have not been aware of it I suppose it must all have come as a bit of a shock. Were you upset? Frightened?'

She hesitated.

'No, not frightened really. It was just—well,

57

I didn't know what was happening and the voice—it wasn't my voice—.'

In cases like this it is always important to find out whether fear or any kind of negative or destructive element is present since this can indicate a mental illness such as paranoid schizophrenia rather than psychic ability. As a general rule of thumb, however, if the attitude and reactions are balanced and positive, the cause is more likely to be psychic than clinical—though in any case that seems doubtful I would always refer the sitter to a doctor. This time, though, I did not think there was any need to worry about my sitter's sanity. I had seen her Guide for myself.

'It seems so unlikely,' she continued bewilderedly. 'You say I have a wonderful gift—and I suppose I have been preparing myself for something like this for years really, but—well, why me? How is it possible I can be so special?'

I smiled at her. This too was a sane response to the situation.

'We all say that when we start off in this kind of work—or we do if we're going to be any good at it. But why not you? Somebody has to be special—and apart from the fact that you have this wonderful ability, you are just like the rest of us, just like everyone else.'

To help her experience the presence of her Guide, I encouraged her to communicate with him while I was there to assist her, rather than wait until she was alone at home. Her face, as it changed, became heavy and distressed. She screwed up her eyes painfully, and when she was able to, she told me:

'I cannot do it, I have experienced this before and it is such a terrible pressure of sadness, I can't bear it. The sadness is always there, but it is so much worse if I try to do something like this.'

Tears began to roll down her cheeks.

'If he is a Native American Indian, he is probably speaking for his people and their history was filled with sadness,' I encouraged. 'Let it through, don't hold on to it. He has things he wants to say—let him say them. The sadness is his, not yours. It can't hurt you.'

She straightened up, suddenly alert, hope brightening her face.

'You mean—I can just let it go, let it all pass? All this sadness—I have always thought it was mine even though I didn't know why it was there or why I was sad. If I don't need to carry it any more, that is wonderful. Is it really all his?'

'You don't have to carry anything that comes through. It is nothing to do with you,' I assured her. 'Whatever your Guide feels, simply let it through. All you are there for is to be the means by which he can speak, to give him a voice.'

The second case occurred when I was staying

59

overnight at the house of a lady called Annette, who had invited me to conduct a working weekend on healing for herself and her friend Molly. Annette had mentioned earlier that she had twice found her bedroom curtains drawn apart when she woke in the morning during the previous week.

'Do you think there is anything significant about that?' she asked me. 'I didn't do it, and the cats play and move the curtains, but they couldn't possibly have drawn them apart so neatly—and certainly not twice. Could someone or something be trying to give me a message?'

At the time my attention was elsewhere and the significance of the drawn curtains was pushed to one side. During the afternoon, however, something else happened. Annette noticed a strange cat in the yard outside her back door, obviously hungry and crying.

'Isn't it yours?' I enquired, for there were three cats in her house and I found them confusing. 'It's a Siamese—I thought I saw it in the kitchen just now.'

'No, I've never seen it before,' she said, but took pity on its obvious state of distress and brought it in for some food, while Molly and I had a look round the adjoining yards and streets to see whether there was any sign of where the cat belonged. It was a beautiful animal, obviously a pedigree.

Neither of the girls had seen it anywhere in

the vicinity before—as we all agreed, you wouldn't exactly forget to notice a cat like that—and there was no indication at all of where it had come from. As the afternoon passed the cat gratefully made itself at home and went to sleep—it was fortunate that it had wandered to a house where there were already three cats and it could be catered for and given temporary shelter. Annette interrupted the work we were doing to notify the police and also the local newspaper's 'Pet Watch' line where the animal was, so that when its owner made enquiries it could be collected. But hours later, no-one had called.

Annette and Molly had begun to wonder whether there was something significant about the cat's appearance.

'Do you think it could be a visitation? Something from the spirit world?' they asked, adding that it reminded them of a Siamese cat that had belonged to a friend who had died in tragic circumstances.

'Maybe, possibly, but first and foremost it is a lost animal that needs to be reunited with its owner, who must be out of his or her head with worry. There's nothing supernatural about that,' I said rather dismissively.

We were relaxing over a meal in the evening when I recollected Annette's words about the drawn curtains in her bedroom and I offered to see whether I could 'pick up' anything there. As soon as I stepped through the door at the top of the stairs, I could feel a presence which I thought was that of a young man, somebody who seemed to have had curly dark hair. It was his spirit which had drawn the curtains to make her realise he was there—possibly also symbolically, to 'get in'.

'He doesn't mean you any harm. He seems rather confused and upset. Does the description mean anything to you?' I asked Annette as we sat down to discuss the 'haunting'.

Annette and Molly agreed it could be the same young man they had mentioned before, the one who had committed suicide and to whom the cat had belonged. I told them that if he had bothered to try to contact Annette, he probably had something to say to her, some message. We went back to the room to find out, if possible, what this was.

As soon as I stepped across the threshold he was there, and I reported to them that he was extremely upset.

'I feel I must comfort him,' I said, instructing them to offer me what support they could as I tried to console the sobbing spirit. In the everyday setting of an ordinary room, it must have been a bizarre experience for them—neither with any previous exposure to this kind of work—as I 'held' the distraught spirit in my arms and soothed it. For the dead man's emotion and distress also passed through me so that tears were streaming down my face and I was shaking violently all the time I was clasping what to them would have looked like empty air and assuring it that 'It's all right, everything is all right now.'

The message that emerged was, I explained to them afterwards, that the young man had 'had no dignity either in his life or in his death.' He needed respect as a person, as an individual. I was not aware of the circumstances of his life and death, but the girls explained that he had been gay and that he had committed suicide by hanging himself with a chain so that his body fell at his lover's feet when his partner entered their flat. His funeral, it appeared, had been loud and blaring with pop music, and there had been no prayers or blessing, no minister present. Even his ashes had never been scattered or buried and so far as they knew, the girls said, were still lying round in the flat where the young man's former partner had started a new relationship.

I was able to complete his message for Annette and Molly—the friends he had entrusted with his request because he believed they would carry it out for him. He wanted a grave, and he wanted flowers placed on it. A sheaf of red carnations. He wanted dignity in his death, not pity and horror at his terrible end. More—he wanted a photograph taken and for them to be able to show it to other people and say: 'This is a picture of Terry's grave.'

The girls were only too eager to comply with his wish and promised to contact everyone concerned and see that it was carried out. We agreed that it had been a most amazing weekend—more especially since, as I pointed out, his spirit had arrived at Annette's house wanting to contact her, on the one occasion when a medium who could pass his message on would be staying there. And he had made his presence known by moving her bedroom curtains—and by sending a Siamese cat.

When I left the girls, I asked them to keep me informed about what happened with regard to 'Nameless' the Siamese, but a week later—having had him checked with a vet, and ascertained that he was not 'tagged'—Annette still had him with her. No-one had yet claimed this beautiful and expensive animal who had come from nowhere.

CHAPTER FOUR

GHOST CASEBOOK

'Can you see ghosts and things?' I get asked often, and for years I used to say rather regretfully that no, I had never seen a ghost. Then I realised that though I still have not 'seen' one with my physical sight, I actually see them all the time with my 'second sight' or inner vision. Or rather, I perceive their presence and can describe and communicate with them—even enter the dimension where they are so that they do not need to materialise physically for me to be aware of them.

What is a ghost, really? According to two pocket dictionaries I have just consulted, a ghost is defined as: 'person's spirit appearing after their death' and 'a spirit, a dead person appearing again, a spectre; a semblance.' In both these cases the emphasis seems to be on the word 'appearing'. Ghosts are generally recognised as beings which are still 'seen' in a physical sense after they have departed to the spirit world—but what exactly is the difference between any departed spirit or even a 'Spirit Guide', and a ghost? They are all (or nearly all) spirit forms of people who have lived on the Earth plane and no longer do so. Departed souls can make contact or pass on their messages through a medium, but are the spirits who are contacted in this way ghosts? Is there a difference?

Since none of us have any first-hand knowledge of life on any other plane than this one—even if we can offer comments based on our own personal spiritual awareness and beliefs—nobody will ever know the full story about ghosts, how and why they occur, until we too have passed on. And different people have different ideas about the spirit world—they are all equally valid if they are what the individual needs at that time. As with all learning processes, concepts of heaven and spirit life can alter as the individual progresses in awareness and spiritual maturity.

It comforts many people to believe that the departed are waiting for them somewhere on the other side of the 'great divide' and that after death they will be reunited and things will go on much the same as they did on the Earth, except that all illness, pain and problems will be wiped out. I am sure that, as with our 'Spirit Guides', our heavens too are personal and will prove to be all we might have desired when we eventually achieve them.

But the concept of a happy-ever-after land beyond the rainbow does not seem to include any future progress, and in my experience death is not an ending to the soul's spiritual journey, simply a gateway into yet another aspect of it. For some souls, all they needed to achieve on the Earth has been done, but many are still young in spiritual learning and need to grow and progress even after death. However—or even whether—this actually happens is for every individual to judge for himself according to his personal belief, but one thing that does seem universally accepted is that once any living being is physically dead, that is that so far as its span of life here is concerned. It no longer belongs on the Earth but somewhere else—whether it may later live some other life is a different story altogether. The current book of life has closed.

And yet, spirits in many forms do return, for whatever reason. 'Spirit Guides' appear to come back prompted by a high order of universal, unconditional love because they want to assist the living. Departed relatives appear to communicate because of their human love for those they have left behind and a desire to reassure and comfort them. When spirits return voluntarily (in whatever shape or form) and this can be said to have occurred in some kind of ordered, recognised manner, they are invariably prompted by some kind of love. If there is something negative or otherwise disjointed about their appearance, they may be some form of ghost. My own personal definition of a ghost, based on my experience of them, is that it is a spirit which has either returned without its own awareness

67

(and probably without love), or else it has never really left.

Many people are confused by the apparent vagueness of all psychic activity and psychic work and want things spelled out for them in black and white. They want to reduce everything to earthly terms, and do not understand that the laws governing the spiritual and psychic planes are different. In many ways I can sympathise with this for at one time, before I was aware of my own 'second sightedness', I was inclined to take this view myself. It is difficult for any intelligent, thinking person, with no experience of how the psychic world works, to appreciate that it has its own recognisable laws and logic which are quite valid even though these do not apparently conform with laws and logic understandable to the human brain.

One of the things that irks people is why, for instance, messages from spirit realms are often not clear. Why does the medium say that a departed spirit is passing on an image of a cake with pink icing on it, which the recipient of the message eventually identifies as a special cake her mother baked for her fifth birthday party, when it would have been far easier for the spirit to have said simply: 'Remember the cake I made for you when you were five? This proves that I am your mother.'

And why do those stalwarts of prediction,

cryptic phrases like 'a journey over water', 'a conflict within', 'beware a dark stranger', continue to be heard when card readings are done? This kind of archaic phraseology has just got to be a cop-out, cynics claim. Why can psychics not say exactly what they mean? It would be far more convenient for everyone—not to mention give psychic activity more credibility in a world suspicious of intangibles like faith and possibility, a world which demands everything spelled out clearly for the consumer, preferably with a guarantee and assurance of money back if not satisfied.

When the psychic refers to journeying over water, conflicts within or a significant person's dark influence in the future, why is he or she not be able to see—and say—that: 'You are going to catch the night ferry to Dublin on Thursday'? Or 'You are going to have to decide whether to leave home and take a job in Nova Scotia where you will be independent but lonely, or stay with your parents and feel resentful because they continue to treat you like a child'—or even 'You are going to meet Ted, a charismatic but untrustworthy employee of the telephone company, when he comes to install a new telephone line.'

The language of imagery in which spirits often communicate, and the cryptic phrases of divination and prophecy, are actually far more precise than 'spelling it out'—so long as you understand how these work. All psychic concepts are open-ended, whereas the human concept is necessarily finite, with the prospect of death hovering somewhere ahead like a gigantic full stop. Psychic vision is a widening of horizons rather than an exploration of boundaries. So it is no wonder that the psychic's avoidance of definitions can be frustrating—and can even be regarded suspiciously as a cover-up for abilities he or she does not possess.

When I began my psychic work I was able to appreciate these differences and, in my role as an interpreter, make them understandable to other people to some extent through my books. But often the principles of a wider existence are impossible to put into words. At one time I found people would ask why, if I was psychic, I did not insist on getting answers from the spirit world to all kinds of questions from the secret of the universe and who God really is, to the winner of every kind of race on which money can be gambled. They also had a habit of saying craftily:

'All right, if you can read people's minds, tell me what I am thinking now.'

But the reason why no reputable psychic will be drawn on this kind of thing is because such challenges only reveal the spiritual immaturity of the challenger. If I am ever asked to 'prove' my psychic abilities I reply that I have no desire to prove them. They are perfectly real to me, but whether other people accept them or not is entirely up to them.

A question I am often asked is some variation on whether I 'really believe in all this psychic stuff.' But it is not a matter of whether I believe in it or not. I live it. I generally reply with a question for the questioner.

'Do you believe you exist and breathe?'

Some people feel obliged to inform me with a regretful shake of their head that: 'I'm sorry, I just can't take any of it, really.'

This at least is honest, though I think they are surprised when I make no effort to defend my position. I never try to convert anyone to my way of living and my personal realities— whatever they want to take or not take is their prerogative. Even when conducting consultations for sitters I often remind them if I feel it is necessary that: 'You do not have to believe anything I say or act on it, if you choose not to. I hope my comments will help you but they are entirely my own personal opinions and convictions, and since only you will ever really know what is best for you, you must in the end use your own judgement and make up your own mind.'

Discriminating souls will often announce that: 'Oh, I'll accept some of this sort of talk, I mean I believe ghosts exist. But as for all the rest, seeing the future and "Spirit Guides", angels and such, no, I can't go along with any of that at all.'

71

But if you accept any part of the principles of psychic existence you must (theoretically, at any rate) accept the whole. You cannot pick and choose, deciding you will take the bits you like but refusing to acknowledge the ones that make you uncomfortable or that you do not understand. It is like trying to claim you accept the physical existence of your lungs because you know you breathe air in and out, but denying the existence of your bowels and sweat glands because you would prefer not to have to admit to any, or your appendix and parts of your brain because they appear to contribute nothing to your existence and you do not know why they are there nor how they work.

The psychic laws on cause and effect are the other way round to physical laws. Whereas in the material world something has to be defined and proved to exist before it is accepted as valid, the laws of psychic activity state that: *'Because* something, however unlikely, has been experienced as existing, then it is valid whether it has been defined and proved or not.'

In my work, I regularly encounter large numbers of departed souls and spirits as well as other kinds of entities. I do not consider any of them 'ghostly' or 'spooky' since I generally have some understanding of why they are there, what they are doing, what they want and how the rules which govern their existence work. For instance, the reason why ghostly phenomena are popularly regarded as frightening—the cold and other physical manifestations encountered in situations where the spirit world is involved—is because they exist in another dimension and on another plane to the physical. It is in the nature of things that the purely physical will always find something from another dimension alien and frightening for many reasons, from the structure of its manifested form to the fact that its existence is actually beyond our physical senses to comprehend.

Interestingly, I have learned that, though I can move easily and routinely into and out of the dimensions where spirits exist, if I was actually to 'see' a ghost myself with my physical eyes, my physical body would react automatically to it. Because it would be a manifestation from one plane to another where it did not belong, I would be made very uneasy and probably even find the experience physically frightening. In the same way as all human beings are programmed to cling instinctively to their physical existence and fear the actual process of dying—though often they have no fear of 'being dead'—they are very uncomfortable in the presence of anything which they know intuitively does not originate on the same human plane as themselves. Even if the visitation is recognised as elevated or spiritually superior, the effect can be the same.

One of the physical signs of other-worldly presence which a psychic learns to recognise is the cold chill on the skin that is such a feature of spooky stories. This actually does occur when there is a visitation from the spirit world. The coldness indicates that the entity or spirit is drawing the physical energy it needs to assist it to descend (or sometimes, ascend) to the Earth plane. Whether or not it materialises in some form in which it may be acknowledged by the physical senses, any entity or spirit still needs to draw energy for a physical existence—however fleeting or temporary—from some suitable source and this is usually the nearest living being.

I feel the familiar tightening of my scalp, crawling skin and cold chill quite often in my work. It alerts me to the fact that a spirit is present, sometimes because I have contacted it on behalf of a sitter, or sometimes because it has come of its own volition and wants to make contact itself.

People are not generally aware that there are many different types of ghosts. The simplest and least complicated occur as a kind of 'echo' from the past, the imprint of a person, scene, incident or emotion left on the ether which can be 'picked up' by a receptive mind in the present. These play no part in events outside of their own time, they carry no message and

74

the ghosts themselves are unaware that their impressions linger. Their spirits are not really here, their appearance is simply a moment of past time repeating itself over and over as a stuck needle on a record might do.

I was invited to read the Tarot cards for several members of the staff at a pub in Newcastle-under-Lyme and we sat in the empty bar. Afterwards Marnie, the landlady, asked me:

'Do you see any ghosts? The building is very old, you know.'

I looked round. The big lounge bar was divided into two sections.

'This part is new,' I said consideringly. 'It's the room through there that's the old part.'

'That's right,' she agreed, rather surprised that I could tell since everywhere looked the same. 'This part has been built on. The bar used to stop there, behind the wall.'

As I looked round, concentrating, I could 'see' a woman standing against the wall and I described her to Marnie.

'A little old lady in a long shabby black skirt and white blouse or shawl, standing there waiting to be served. But if this part of the bar did not exist then, I don't know why she is waiting there. She's in the wrong place. She would have been standing outside the pub.'

Marnie smiled and told me that the ghost of the little old lady had been seen on many occasions by many different people in that same spot. Apparently the wall where she was standing had once been the serving window where the locals came to have their jugs of ale filled without actually having to enter the bar.

I turned my attention to the other, older part of the room. As I stared into the empty modern lounge with its silent tables and chairs I began to 'pick up' another scene of great activity superimposed upon it, as though one transparency was being laid on another.

'There is a well under this room I think, and a cellar. I can see a trapdoor—or some sort of trap thing—it is open and there are steps going down.'

The scene clarified itself in amazing detail. I described to Marnie how: 'The floor is about eighteen inches lower than the floor is now, and it seems like it is made of packed earth. The room is dim, the light is flickery and it's very smoky. It's full of men, I think some of them were sailors—seamen. They seem to be playing some sort of game on the floor and there are little dogs running about.'

The picture was a fascinating one. I could see the whole of the main room of the public house in another era which I thought was vaguely late Victorian though I could not be sure. Marnie confirmed that this was an accurate description of what the scene would have looked like in the past. Those former drinkers, accompanied by their whippet dogs, would have been engaged in playing skittles.

Especially interesting was that though this particular pub was nowhere near the sea—or even near a large river—and I could not explain why I had the impression the men were sailors, I learned that the canal had at one time passed by the site and this had been a noted meeting place for the watermen and bargees.

On another occasion Paul and I were talking quite casually about one of the properties in the street where he lived. We had known each other twenty years before and lost touch but, as I mentioned earlier, had renewed our friendship in 1997 when I contacted Paul and passed on Brother Gregory's channelled messages. I had commuted between London and the Midlands to be with him while he underwent an operation and recuperated from it, and when we found we did not want to be parted again I left London to be with him permanently.

The house where I now lived was semi-detached with a long garden, in a suburban road a mile outside Newcastle-under-Lyme in Staffordshire. The properties along it were prosperous and pleasant, but one of them affected me badly. I explained to Paul that the reason I disliked it was because:

'When I look through the gate as I'm going by, I don't seem to see the house and grounds at all. I get the impression of something that

77

looks like a battlefield after a terrible massacre, empty and devastated and awful with debris, fires burning themselves out, threads of smoke, that kind of thing. It has a horrible atmosphere, really upsetting.'

It was some time later, after he had thought about my words, that Paul told me the house in question had been built on the site of a former small-holding where a number of animals, including pigs, had been kept. He did not of course remember the event himself, but his mother had heard stories of how in the late 1920s there had been an outbreak of swine fever among the pigs. They had all had to be slaughtered, and the carcasses had been burned and buried on the land now occupied by the house and gardens I found so uncomfortable.

In this case, it was obvious that the emotional as well as the visual traces of the event still lingered. After Paul had told me about the slaughter of the pigs, I recalled how I had experienced a similar atmosphere in the 1960s when I had had to travel regularly by bus along the main road from Wrexham to Chester, where I lived and worked at that time. For weeks I had seen the awful sight of smoke rising from fires as whole herds of cattle, victims of the terrible outbreak of Foot and Mouth Disease that had devastated the country, were slaughtered where they stood and their piled bodies burned in deep pits in their own fields before the remains could be buried.

On a more cheerful note, I encountered an unexpected ghost one Christmas when I had been invited to spend Boxing Day with a family in London. I did not know them well and had never visited their house before, but was made very welcome and after a wonderful meal we all sat round relaxing and enjoying the good company and the conversation. I mentioned that I could 'see' the image of a little animal in a corner of the room near the big French doors that opened onto the garden (now shut, of course, since it was the middle of winter). It was obviously the ghost of some loved and long departed pet, though I did not get the impression that it was trying to pass on any message. It seemed to be quite unaware that it was there.

'Did you have a pet cat or pet dog ever?' I asked, and described the little creature. 'It's small with soft fur, black and white—white with black patches, I think.'

But though they had always had pets, no-one in the family could recollect a small animal that had been black and white. The departed dogs had been large ones, a golden retriever and a spaniel, and the cats had been a grey Persian and several patchwork moggies. After fruitless discussion, they suggested reluctantly that perhaps this particular pet had lived at some previous time in the house's history.

'Well, maybe. But are you sure you can't place it? I can see it so clearly. It is definitely black and white, small, soft and furry. Too big for a kitten—a puppy perhaps—.' Suddenly inspired, I added the information that: 'It had drooping ears, soft drooping ears.'

Breakthrough! At the mention of its ears one of the daughters of the house suddenly exclaimed excitedly: 'Flopsy? He had black patches. Could it be Flopsy?'

Apparently Flopsy had been a flop-eared rabbit which had been a pet when the children were very young. Once they had remembered his existence the family members were able to tell me how he used to roam freely in the garden, and come in through the French doors when they were open in summer. His favourite place had been the corner of the big living-room where I could 'see' him. The mystery was solved, though why a flop-eared rabbit should make such an impression on the ether that his ghost was still there years later at a Boxing Day dinner, I have no idea.

Though ghosts of the type I have detailed above are entirely unaware, simply impressions on the ether which do not really exist, there are other occasions where a part of the personality has become trapped or stuck, often in a moment of particularly strong emotion. In such cases the spirits cannot move on until someone takes the appropriate action to free them. Ghosts of this type do not appear to have had any choice over whether they became trapped or not, and though it is popularly believed that phantoms are present because of some incident of heavy trauma like murder, this need not always be the case.

Judy worked at a hair salon where I was having my hair styled. As she shampooed and cut, she told me she was having a problem with the new flat she had just moved into. There was 'something' in the bedroom that made the atmosphere cold and unpleasant and, several times at night, she had woken up to see the luminous figure of a woman standing beside the bed.

'It's haunted?' I said, but Judy set her jaw grimly. She did not believe in ghosts, she told me. Nevertheless, things were getting out of hand. Her boyfriend had also woken the previous night and seen the ghostly figure. Less tough than Judy, he had been so shaken that he was not anxious to repeat the experience. So much against her principles, Judy invited me to visit the flat to see what I could do.

I was able to 'pick up' the spirit of a young woman in the bedroom—an adolescent, I thought, probably about fourteen or fifteen. She was trapped in a single instant of time when she had been shaken with a fit of hysterical crying, though what she had been crying about did not seem relevant. I thought it had probably been with temper over something quite trivial rather than because of any deep, painful emotion like grief or despair.

I 'spoke' to the spirit—rather sharply to gain its attention and shake it out of its preoccupation with itself—then pointed out to it that there was no longer any reason for it to keep on crying. I instructed it to leave and go home to the Light where it belonged rather than continue to remain earthbound. Once communication has been made and the ghost can be persuaded to understand its plight, there is generally no problem in seeing it on its way. The girl's spirit left the flat through the front door which, as in all cases like this, I had symbolically opened. When she had gone—again as I always do—I prayed for her and instructed Judy and her boyfriend Del to burn a candle for her spirit and lay fresh flowers in the cold spot in the bedroom where the ghost image had been appearing.

The chilly atmosphere—often due to emotional negativity as well as spirit presence—was already beginning to clear and Judy seemed relieved. A few weeks later when I saw her again, however, she surprised me by behaving as though the incident had never happened. This kind of reaction can be quite common, particularly if the individuals concerned do not want to accept the evidence of their own senses regarding extra-ordinary phenomena, even when these are actually taking place. Some people's ability to delude themselves in this way can be almost farcical.

Rob, a television producer who came for a reading in London, was very overworked and stressed. I suggested he took a holiday, preferably somewhere in the sun.

'I have a villa in Spain,' he said rather grudgingly. 'But I can't go there any more. My first wife is there and she makes it very difficult for me and for Sara (his present wife).'

Since he had already told me his first wife was dead I found this a little confusing.

'Sorry, I thought you said she had died in an accident. She recovered, then, and she lives at the villa?' I queried. He stared at me, frowning as though irritated.

'Of course she didn't recover. I've just explained to you, she fell from the cliffs in a place where there are rocks below. It was actually while we were at the villa, that was where it all happened.'

'Oh, I see. So it's her ghost which is haunting the villa. That is very sad. Have you tried to get someone to help her to leave, to move on?'

'Haunting the villa? What a shocking thing to suggest,' Rob said as though scandalised. 'I do not believe in such things as ghosts. My first wife is just being awkward and trying to make

83

sure Sara and I can't enjoy ourselves together. She was always inclined to be jealous. I would rather not discuss her attitude if you don't mind.'

I never found out how he resolved this particular marital triangle.

Sometimes spirits will remain close to the Earth plane until a task or errand has been completed to their satisfaction. Paul told me that in the course of his work as a horticulturist, he had spent some years restoring the grounds of a house that had once belonged to the founder of a famous pottery firm. He became aware that the spirit of the old gentleman (though at first he did not know who it was) was watching him as he worked. The ghost continued to appear at regular intervals for over two years while the restoration went on. It was not until it had been completed—including restoring a large rockery the old man had created years before to its former beauty—that the ghost was willing to leave the garden he had loved.

In many cases it appears that ghostly activity finds a focus in certain places or where certain people are present, and they seem to congregate. Sometimes it is the original energy that attracts the rest or even, in extreme cases, causes them to happen. And there are ghosts that continue to play an active part in the events of the present, just as though they were still living.

Patricia, a busy career woman who worked in a shop in the town, stopped me one day and asked me whether I would visit her small terraced house. It was haunted, she said. A ghostly man kept appearing in the middle of the night and she would feel the movement of her bed in the dark as he 'sat' on the edge of it and leaned over her.

While we were speaking, I 'picked up' the figure she was talking about. I thought it was that of a soldier, or at least, someone wearing a soldier's greatcoat. I asked whether she had lost a relative who had been in the First or Second World War, a grandfather perhaps, since I thought the spirit was one known to her, but she said she could not identify it so I agreed to call and see what I could do.

When I inspected her house I noted that there was an intensely cold area in the kitchen in spite of the warmth of the comfortable gas fire. Patricia agreed that it would never warm up even if the heat was on very high, adding:

'When I sit in that spot, my legs and feet go numb after only a short while. It has always been like that, ever since I bought the house.'

I could 'see' that there was a woman present, sitting down in that part of the room looking out of the window. She had her coat on ready to go out. I told Patricia she had been a woman who had lived in the house previously and who had not wanted to leave it.

'She sat here in the few minutes before she went out for the last time, just looking round and feeling a terrible wrench that she would never see it again, holding on to her memories of all the happy years she had spent here. And then somebody called her and she got up and went out into the car, or whatever it was that took her away. She must have lived somewhere else afterwards, and died there. But part of her never left this room. It is still here and I must make contact with her, tell her that she can't stay here any longer and help her to leave.'

Using the same methods I had used with Judy's distraught adolescent girl I 'spoke' to the woman and reassured her that it was time to move on now, time to go home. I accompanied her spirit to the open front door, watching as she eventually left. We prayed for her and Patricia placed a candle on the floor with some flowers I had brought with me in case they should be needed. When I saw her the following week she told me the cold atmosphere in the kitchen had completely gone.

'It's really lovely and cosy now. I have my coffee sitting there by the table and last night I was there for ages doing a jigsaw when I realised suddenly that my feet and legs hadn't frozen up as they usually do, they were still warm. It's amazing,' she said. She had also made enquiries among the neighbours and thought she had identified the woman.

'Someone who lived in the house and left in about the 1960s, a few occupants back. She'd come as a bride years before and been there all her married life and raised her children. When she and her husband left she didn't want to go and was apparently dreadfully upset when they moved out. I think that must have been her, don't you?'

This, of course, had not been the problem about which she had consulted me in the first place. So what of the ghostly man who had been appearing in Patricia's bedroom? She told me that my description of the soldier in the greatcoat had solved the mystery even before my visit.

'I suddenly remembered one of my uncles. He was a soldier, he died very young, and I never knew him. But as soon as I realised it was him, I knew somehow that he had been trying to give me a message and what it was. He wanted to tell me that everything was going to be all right with the problems I have been having to do with the family.' She smiled. 'And once I realised who it was and that he was trying to give me help and support, I knew that *he* knew that I had got the message, and he would not come back again. And he hasn't been.'

When I went up to her room just to check after we had dealt with the sad lady who did not want to leave her kitchen, I was able to confirm that Patricia was right. There was no sensation of any ghostly activity there at all.

I found when I came to live with Paul that though I had no idea of it beforehand, I was moving into a house where there were several ghosts in residence. I had already told him on the phone that I could sense the presence of his mother, who had died a few years previously, and Paul confided that he had seen her himself. One day when his mind was entirely on other things, he had come down the stairs to find her inspecting some new curtains that had just been hung, examining the thickness of the material in her fingers.

'She was there for a fraction of a second and then—gone,' he told me.

In the months while I settled in, I realised that there was a great deal of ghostly activity in the house. At first I assumed it was all emanating from the same spirit, though I was surprised to find that much of it was depressing and threatening, inducing a kind of mental paralysis against which I had to struggle hard. I had never actually met Paul's mother but he did not have to tell me that she had been a strong-willed and determined lady—I came to know her spirit well. She tested me constantly, coming up behind me and 'leaning' heavily on my shoulder to see how much of this sort of pressure I could take. I think she was trying to see how far she could push me before I ran gibbering from the house—she would obviously have had no time for a weak-kneed successor in what she still considered her domain.

Sometimes, even though I knew Paul was also aware of her presence, I wondered whether I was over-reacting to life in an environment that was very different to the psychic circles I had been used to in London. But one evening when the milkman came as he did every week to collect the milk money, he told Paul, rather white in the face, that:

'I have just seen your mother looking out of the window when I knocked on the front door.'

Apparently it had always been Paul's mother's custom to lean out of that same window to pay the milkman when she was alive.

I did a great deal of work with this independent ghost, explained to her that she had died and must move on the way she was to go. I pointed out that she was free now to soar out of the confinement of the physical. If she wanted to, she could even pursue ambitions that had been thwarted in her life—she had longed for a career as a fashion designer. Furniture that had belonged to her was sold and the rooms of the house reorganised. Yet still she would not leave, though she learned (rather grudgingly, I felt) to respect me.

After completing a healing session recently, I left the room to make a drink. When I returned to my patient (who had come to me in great distress fearing she might be going

89

mad, but typically was actually extremely psychic), she told me:

'As you went out, two other people came in. And as soon as you came back in, they went out again.'

She described them. 'I think they were two women. One was strong, but not so strong as you. The other was just sort of trotting after her.'

I knew the first ghost well, of course, but the second was rather a surprise. However, I 'picked up' the image and later described it to Paul. 'A small, slight sort of person, with glasses.'

He considered. 'It sounds like Laura. My mother's best friend.'

So I concluded with amusement that even ghosts can sometimes feel the need to call in reinforcements.

I identified a second presence in the house apart from Paul's mother. It was this that had caused the dismal, densely paralysing atmosphere that made it hard for me when I first arrived. It still remains, lurking unsuspected to prey on any sign of negativity. Far more basic than a spirit, it is a dark coil of energy that seeps up like thick and greasy smoke out of the ground on which the house is built.

Energies like this have no cause as such, they attach themselves wherever they are allowed to do so and cannot actually be sent home to the Light for they are, to whatever degree, fragments of the Dark. They can be cleared from places they inhabit, but only move on to somewhere else. I believe this particular energy helped contribute to keeping Paul's mother earth-bound, and I know it would do the same to any other spirit—to him, to me—if it could.

The ghosts I encountered when I first came here are still present in the house. I feel that, in this case, the final decisions are not mine to make—sometimes the psychic worker must allow families to resolve their on-going affairs (whether material or spiritual) between themselves.

CHAPTER FIVE

THE DARK SIDE

Possessing psychic potential means that each day and the happenings in it can be a minefield. The old word to describe a psychic—a 'sensitive'—expresses this best, for the psychic person's acute sensitivity to all the energies around him means he will be far more open to dark or negative influences than a less psychically gifted person. You cannot be 'partly psychic'. You either are psychically aware or you are not—and if you are, you have to be ready to protect yourself if this should be necessary since you cannot know what you are going to encounter at any given time.

I am not speaking now of encounters of the kind portrayed in films and books like *The Exorcist* and *The Amityville Horror*. Scenarios of this nature and intensity very rarely take place even in the life of a professional psychic and often, extra-ordinary situations which seem frightening and threatening to those affected by them can be explained and dealt with quite easily by someone who is familiar with this kind of phenomenon.

In actual fact, only a relatively small percentage of supposed ghostly, spooky or other psychic activity comes from the psychic world. Much can be explained away by natural causes—the movement of water, particularly underground, for instance, can have a strange effect on surrounding areas. The natural rhythms of the tides, the influence of the waxing and waning of the moon—these have been recognised and proved by reputable authorities to cause strange, often inexplicable happenings both to inanimate things and to people. Sounds, strange lights, shadows, smells, however weird and bizarre, are often of natural origin.

Yet a further percentage of seemingly supernatural phenomena are some form of physical manifestation of the state of mind of people involved with them. Extreme mental pressure and stress, repressed anger, frustration or fear can heighten awareness and the physical energies to a point far beyond the norm. The activities of poltergeists often fall within this category, and in most cases of poltergeist activity there will be a human source, often an adolescent though the person can be any age. What matters is the highly charged state of mind that seems to trigger off apparently supernatural and often violent physical activity in the vicinity, which an experienced worker in this field learns to recognise. Though I have never been asked to investigate a case of this kind myself I have had some experience of such states of mind and the resulting kinds of energy, and they can be very threatening and frightening. It is difficult to be comfortable or feel safe around such people, whatever the actual circumstances, yet they are the ones who are most frightened and upset and in need of help.

All dark and frightening supernatural activity is made worse when one is afraid of it. Negative energy feeds on fear. Some understanding of this can immediately reduce any apparently terrifying situation to more manageable proportions—though it has to be admitted, it does take something away from the popular mystique that surrounds spooky stories and 'Tales of the Uncanny'. People love to be frightened when they are in a safely controlled situation. It is when they feel they have no control and are out of their depth that fear stops being pleasurable.

In psychic work one becomes familiar with different energies and gets used to dealing with them. Just as a deep sea diver can accustom himself to the water pressures in the depths of the ocean and learn to adjust his mental and physical reactions accordingly, or an astronaut can learn to cope with being weightless, a psychic can recognise changes in the natural energies around him and work within them without being intimidated by them. Mostly, they cause no harm if they are recognised, accepted and handled appropriately, though there are some occasions when it is difficult to maintain a cool head since even experienced psychic workers can find themselves in the realms of the unknown.

One psychic described to me the kind of energy she had encountered in a house that was built on the crossing of two 'ley lines'. The whole building hummed and vibrated with mysterious force. It was quite uninhabitable and the owners were in despair for they could neither live in it nor sell it. They complained that they were thrown down the stairs if they tried to go up to the first floor, and could not enter the dining-room at all.

'I stood in the doorway and the whole room and everything in it seemed to be flickering in and out of existence like a picture on a giant TV screen,' my friend reported. 'There were lines across it and the power kept slowly working its way down the lines. It was incredible. I did not dare to go into the room.'

Three other psychics I worked with were called in to try and rid a pub of whatever was causing the disruptions the staff were experiencing, though these seemed to be at least partly the result of human tragedy rather than caused by energy fields. One visitor staying at the pub had hung himself in his room and his ghost apparently walked on the top floor. But there was poltergeist activity in the basement too, most recently where an iron and ironing board had been picked up by an unseen hand and thrown violently down a corridor at a terrified maid, hitting her head. There was also some kind of atmosphere within the building that caused people to start behaving in bizarre ways that were quite out of character.

The attempts of the three psychics to clear the pub were featured in a local paper and a photographer was there to take pictures. But in spite of their efforts the energies within the building simply shifted their focus. The ghost of the hanged man, when instructed to leave peacefully, was seen instead to run violently down the stairs and disappear into the cellars; the iron and ironing board continued to be thrown around with great force. The highly charged atmosphere did not diminish but intensified, as I found when I experienced an uncomfortable evening at the pub myself. Instead of being able to participate in the Psychic Fair in the Function Room, I spent the whole time sitting in a corner in a state of terrible melancholy, fighting off the urge to throw myself from the balcony of the long window beside me. Afterwards I realised that I had been 'picking up' the imbalance of mind of the man who had hanged himself.

When my first psychic book *A Psychic's Casebook* was published in 1995 it was reviewed in the Spiritualist newspaper *Psychic News*. The reviewer made the comment that: 'In the case of those self-satisfied clairvoyants who glibly tell people they are about to die or have a demon on their shoulder, psychological damage must be a real danger. Fortunately, Ms Gater comes across as level-headed enough to meet claims of "devil possession" with a look at the person's life and overall attitude, rather than with a handy vial of holy water.'

Popular tradition as immortalised in the books of Dennis Wheatley and more recently the writers of best-selling horror novels—as well as most media treatment of psychic subjects—insists on representing all psychic activity as largely concerned with dark and sinister magical confrontations with evil incarnate in its most repulsive forms. These are spectacularly inaccurate. Most psychics are decent, ordinary people who because of their 'extra senses' are very aware of the presence and wonder of the divine. Because they are careful to protect themselves with prayers and symbolic evocations of higher power in the form of a cross, an ankh or whatever they feel represents their own particular belief best, they very rarely encounter evil incarnate and most of them do not dabble with magic, dark or otherwise.

You need to keep a level head when you are doing psychic work—not because you will be tempted to fly off into realms of hysterical fancy, but because that is what a large percentage of the general public is inclined to do. In fact one of the best and wisest definitions of spiritual wisdom I have ever encountered is that it is basically nothing but common sense.

But though I try to keep all my activities free from unnecessary theatricality and sensationalism, I have to admit that on some occasions I do need to resort to what I call my 'black bag'. I keep this ready in case the need should arise, packed with a few items I do not normally require for consultations. These include salt, sage, candles, my crucifix and—yes, I'm afraid so—a small bottle which contains water I collected myself from one of the loveliest and most blessed places I know, the well at a shrine to Saint Bridget on the west coast of Ireland. For however practical an attitude one takes, there are some cases where whatever is occurring cannot be explained away except by admitting quite factually that it is caused by the presence of some mischievous or harmful spirit, elemental or sometimes demonic.

On such occasions I am very aware personally that I might be required to confront evil incarnate, and the tools which are used to defend oneself against the Dark are the same ones that have always been used since the beginning of time. Symbols of the power of the elements of earth, air, fire and water. Salt and sage represent cleansing, clearing and purification. Candles represent light and the element of fire, which is also purifying as well as transformational. The sacred water might just as well be from the River Jordan or the Ganges, for what matters is the fact that it is recognised as sacred and consecrated to some form of higher power which is positive and enlightened. Links with this higher power—the fifth element of Spirit—are the most vital weapon of all in any dealing with evil. I happen to believe in the power of the crucifix, but others could just as well use an ankh, a Star of David, the name of Allah or whatever else they feel they can call on to protect themselves.

I did not make any conscious decision to start dealing with cases involving elemental spirits and demons. Indeed, when I began my psychic career I was inclined to take quite a hard line if other people mentioned such things. As the reviewer for *Psychic News* noted, I recounted cases in my book of supposed 'devil possession' which I had treated as ignorance, hysteria, fright, discouragement and general frustration. But I found as I progressed that I was thrown in, as it were, to situations where—whether I had personally accepted their existence or not—elemental and demonic spirits were present and I had to deal with them.

I found myself actually confronting chilly, hostile, mocking, threatening spirits and entities which, if not the extreme evil manifestations that stalk horror movies, were nevertheless most definitely denizens of the Dark. I found too that I experienced the same sense of inadequacy and amazed disbelief I had felt when the Gatekeeper showed me the suffering souls on the plain of red mud. Any ordinary individual suddenly discovering himself or herself in such an extra-ordinary situation would have felt the same. I was—and still am—very aware of my personal limitations.

Fortunately I have always been given the insight and strength to cope effectively but I do not take such incidents lightly or as 'just another case for Super-psychic'. I have learned never to volunteer to venture unasked into situations where such disruptive or destructive manifestations are known or suspected. I believe that as with the wounded souls, any evil will find its way to me without my seeking it out, if or when I need to face it. And though so far I have not encountered anything beyond my strength, it may well be that I will need all the resources I can summon on some future occasion. Spiritual teaching tells us that we are never tested beyond our endurance, but sometimes it can seem frighteningly as though we are way out of our depth.

Though moments of psychic confrontation and heavy trauma do occasionally happen, the real problems psychics have to deal with are far less confrontational. When you are able to 'pick up' on people round you, their negative emotions like hate, anger and fear can sometimes knock you over and blot you out completely. So part of the psychic's training and education is to learn how to protect himself against such massive threats to the personality and any kind of 'psychic attack', whether this is deliberate or happens by accident. He also needs to learn—and at a very early stage if possible—how to 'switch off' his psychic awareness, and how to let such things as do penetrate his defences pass through without harm.

One can never be prepared for everything. I have had several experiences where, as soon as I took hold of the hands of my sitters (all, so far in such cases, women), I felt an electric shock run up my arms. Not just the slight tingling sensation one sometimes gets with healing energies, but a distinct and unpleasantly nasty shock. When the psychic is off guard—and even if the attack, whatever it is, is not deliberate—the effect can be extremely unsettling.

At one big Psychic Fair I attended in Chelsea Town Hall, I found myself during the course of a reading beginning to speak extremely loudly and quickly, interrupting the halting words of my sitter in a very rude, impatient manner. I pointed this out to her, adding:

'It is not the way I normally speak, but I am picking up what you are feeling. This is your own impatience, your own self trying to assert its rights, coming to the surface and confronting you.'

Since she had been married for nearly twenty years and was just beginning to question her husband's cold, selfish attitude and want something back from life except a constant contributing to the well-being of others, she was able to accept this and identify with it.

Two other sitters I saw on the same occasion were Jill and Lee, both young, blonde, sun-tanned. They were friends. Lee proved an unexpectedly advanced soul, on her way to the end of her learning process on the earth with the light of wisdom and unflinching acceptance all around her. But when I took Jill's hands I began to feel my heart pounding in fast, thick beats and my whole nervous system at screaming pitch, shaking with tension, my mind filling with fear.

Since I had suffered from this condition in the past myself, I was able to comment on it and advise Jill to get medical help. But the trouble is that once any kind of negativity has penetrated the barriers it will stay with the psychic unless cleared, and this can be difficult to do if one is tired or (as it always does) the negative energy has latched onto negativity already there.

There are many ways in which a psychic or sensitive person can become 'possessed', and the most common is not by devils or spirits, but by the emotions that emanate from other people. As a child and, indeed, as a young woman I had no real awareness of my psychic powers and was consequently unable to control them or to protect myself from negative energies I picked up all around me. The times when I collapsed, completely unable to carry on, and had to retreat into hospital suffering from 'nervous exhaustion' were classic cases of the healer or psychic's state of 'burn-out'. Attempts to avoid confrontations, actually physically running away, which I was driven to do many times when I was unable to cope, happened because I knew inside that I did not have the strength to try and confront the combined force of anger, disappointment, distress and pain caused to others which would have hit me if I had stayed.

I must have suffered all my life from the presence of fear, anger and frustration in those around me, not knowing—as the transfiguration medium at the Buxton Fair did not know—that I was trying to carry heavy negative emotions that were not my own, not knowing how to avoid the terrible effect on myself. I had no idea that my 'sensitivity' was anything more than average.

Such strong feelings do not even have to be

directed personally against another individual. Psychic or 'sensitive' people will 'pick up' whatever happens to be in the vicinity and unless able to protect themselves, will suffer as a result. The threat may not even be as definite as a feeling or emotion.

In the early days after I met Richard, I became aware that in the following of his own spiritual path he was undergoing much dark and painful struggling within himself. Without revealing his identity, I mentioned to an acquaintance I had met through the Spiritualist Church, and whose opinion I valued, that there was someone I wanted to help. I showed her a snapshot that had been taken in a passport booth.

After studying his face for a moment she said gravely:

'This man has a heavy *karma*, a terribly heavy *karma*. Don't even try to carry it for him. He can carry it—he must—but it would kill you.'

At the time, I was impressed by her sober, matter of fact words. As the years passed, I became more and more aware of how true they had been.

All energy, psychic as well as physical, is in itself neither good nor bad. It becomes positive or negative depending on the use that is made of it. All psychic power is simply there. It may be used just as effectively for good or for evil, and if this is not understood, disaster may result.

There is a rather cryptic saying among psychics that 'Ignorance is no excuse.' Many of the most frightening situations encountered both by genuine psychics and thrill-seekers who 'mess about' with the spirit world are caused inadvertently—mostly with no real desire to hurt anyone—but the effects are exactly the same as though they had been specifically engineered to cause harm. This is why it is such a mistake for anyone to meddle with ouija boards or spells if they have no good reason for it and do not know what they are doing. For if any damage is done, it cannot be undone and it is too late to do anything but try to deal with the situation that has arisen as best one can. In most cases this means calling in outside help.

Eleanor, a lady in her seventies, phoned me to ask whether I would visit her house for a consultation. She said she was depressed and had relationship problems but that was all. Something—my 'sixth sense'—prompted me to take my 'black bag' though I would not usually have taken it to do a reading, and when I arrived at her house I discovered that though she was unaware of it, the building was being haunted by an unpleasant little elemental spirit.

She told me that she was very lonely, and in an attempt to catch herself a man, she had consulted a spell-worker who had come to see her and brought her a spell. But it had not worked. She had not managed to catch the man she wanted, someone else had got him and now she was lonelier than ever because even the few friends she had would no longer come to see her. She had become so depressed that she had been contemplating suicide. Tearfully, she asked me why she was in such a plight. Was someone else casting some other spell, directing it against her?

I could 'see' that the cause of the immediate trouble was crouched on the rug in her living-room in front of the large, luxurious settee, eyeing me balefully. It was an elemental spirit, a dark entity that looked something like a gargoyle, which I soon ascertained had entered the house with the spell-worker when Eleanor had invited him in to deliver her spell. The sad details of this case were typical of many where psychic infestation or even possession can occur.

'I am afraid that both you and this young man were acting out of greed and self-interest,' I told her. 'He was obviously not very skilled at controlling the powers he claimed to possess, or those he was trying to work with. And he wanted your money. You just wanted a man, I know, but it was for purely selfish reasons rather than a genuine attempt to make a true friend and get to know and respect someone else as an individual. You were not willing to make any effort yourself, you wanted a quick fix, a short cut. And because neither of you bothered to take the matter seriously, or protect yourselves when you opened up the channels to the spirit world and invited outside powers in, you let in something you did not expect and which neither of you could cope with. It has been here ever since, it has found itself a comfortable place and is really making itself at home here in your room, feeding on your energy. But naturally, all the friends who used to come here have been driven away now by its coldness and nastiness.'

The elemental spirit was unwilling to leave Eleanor's cosy fireside but eventually I managed to move it, and I watched it depart the house. When I left her, the rooms were all purified, cleared of their depressing atmosphere and cleansed, with candles burning.

We had had a long talk and she had had to face up to the realities of her situation. She was strong, she could and would cope with her depression and her loneliness through her own efforts if she determined to tackle her problems positively and constructively. She did not need to resort to spells to solve her problems. Spells and magic have their place but it is not to help people side-step or dodge their personal responsibilities.

'You are free of the Dark now,' I told her. 'Unless you invite it back or open the way for it to re-enter. The rest is up to you.'

CHAPTER SIX

PAST LIVES AS ANIMALS

During the months while I was still coming to terms with my psychic abilities, I had several sessions of regression to past lives under hypnosis with a practitioner called Lawrence, who also became a friend. These notes, which I made immediately after one of the sessions, describe a previous life I seem to have lived as a cat:

I was aware of being on a level with boots, leggings, a kind of gaiters, the type of thing farm workers or labourers wore a hundred, two hundred years ago. They seemed very big. I suppose they were dirty, smelly, but I didn't seem to notice. There was sawdust, I think, on the floor.

I went out into what must have been a street, but I was not aware that it was a street. There were tall buildings, very tall they seemed to me, sort of pointed, and they seemed to lean across and meet at the top, like looking at something through a round bottle glass. The colours were vague. I had the impression it was dark or everything was a kind of sepia, a yellowy brown.

I had the most incredible sensation of peace. I knew I was thin and had to scavenge for food and I was likely to get kicked by the boots, but I knew somehow that everything was all right. It was like being held in a great big warm hand. I knew that whatever happened to me, everything would be all right.

I suppose you could say—can I joke, since this was a cat?—well, it was purr-fect. Perfect faith, perfect trust and love. I had them all. I did not need anything else. It was one of the most wonderful experiences I have ever known. Utterly simple, but something the human brain cannot even begin to understand. I was just there, and I knew without even knowing that I knew or being able to express it, that I was supposed to be there and I was being looked after, and in spite of it all, everything would be all right.

I noted what occurred exactly as I experienced it, though later I was able to identify details the cat had not been able to appreciate. The place with sawdust on the floor had been a public house bar and the street had been a city street, probably in the Victorian period.

At that time I was still finding my way, struggling to discover myself spiritually. I was not prepared to accept anything blindly—and I still continue to question and consider, to examine all aspects rather than jump to supernatural conclusions. But during the same session I also regressed to previous lives both as a man and a woman, and each gave me insight into the problems of my current existence and helped me come to terms with aspects of myself I had always found difficult to cope with.

As to whether I had actually lived those lives physically in the past or not, I found as so many of my sitters do now that this seemed irrelevant. My experience of them during regression gave me new understanding and new perspectives, so they were most certainly real and valid so far as I was concerned. In a collection of opinions called *Reincarnation: Fact or Fable?* which presents arguments both for and against the theory, I came across this comment by Shigeru Cato, Professor of Philosophy and Religion at the Tokyo University of Art and Design. This seems to express what most people really feel about the subject:

'—in conformity with my pure reason, I reject (the concept of *samsara* or reincarnation) but on the other hand, in the depth of my primitive feelings or unconscious, I believe in (it)!—.'

It did not surprise me that I might have lived other lives or that I might have been male as well as female. But previous existence as a cat was, I admit, unexpected though as with all spiritual and mystical revelations it seemed completely natural. Corroborative evidence would have made it even more interesting and I made enquiries to try and discover whether some of the details could be verified: for

110

instance I had 'seen' with the cat's eyes in a different way to the way I normally saw the world with my human sight.

I wondered whether cats' eyes do actually function like that, so the effect is 'like looking at something through a round bottle glass' and tall buildings seem to lean towards each other and meet at the top. But no-one, even the authorities on animals in the institutions I approached—zoos and universities, seemed to know.

Yet proof of the validity of my experience was not necessary. Nothing, however scientific and convincing, could have explained away the sense of rightness and truth that had been inherent in my regression to my cat-life. It had been incredibly positive and uplifting. I had known what it was like to be completely free from all my human doubts and fears, to be aware with the soul of that thin little animal that I had a place in the scheme of things, that I was personally known to the great power which understood what it was all about and that in the end, whatever happened, it would be what had rightfully been intended to happen.

Fatalistic, this might seem, cynical even. It is often argued that if everything is preordained there can be no point in human struggle or effort to better any situation. It will seemingly all come to the same thing in the end whether we try or don't try, whether we care or not.

111

But this generalisation seems to miss the whole point of existence. If we were here solely to act out, robot-like, some pre-set scenario we would never experience transcending emotions like love, faith, joy, trust. Miracles would never happen—and they do. There is far more to living that just taking what is handed out to us, not caring either way. Yet paradoxically it is the spirit in which we accept our lot that can really transform our lives and those of others.

I thought often about my regression to life as a cat, as well as to the man and the woman I had been in the past, when I started to work as a psychic and become familiar with past and future as an integral part of the present. I learned as my work progressed that all past life experience, however it is obtained, can be meaningful and indeed therapeutic. Accounts of many of the cases I have dealt with and a more detailed analysis of the subject appeared in my book *Past Lives: Case Histories Of Previous Existence*.

Since I had never heard of anyone else who had recollections of any kind about life in animal form, though, I assumed at first that my cat experience was unusual if not unique. However as I began to work with regression myself, conducting sessions for the benefit of sitters who came to consult me, I found rather to my surprise that animal lives soon began to appear alongside the more usual human ones. They seemed to be completely random, in no particular chronological or other recognisable sequence, and they were impossible to predict—I never knew when they might occur. When they did, however, I found that the sitters in question accepted them just as I had done myself and gained as much insight from them as from more traditional past lives as men or women.

I must explain that I do not always regress sitters who want to explore their past lives using hypnosis, as most of the practitioners in this field do. It is not necessary for them to go into a hypnotic trance so that they can regress themselves. By concentrating and focussing my mind I am able to 'link in' and pick up their previous lives, which I then describe to them. At first this method only seemed effective if I did the 'linking in' while holding both the sitter's hands but as time passed I found I could conduct regression sessions without the need of physical contact. Many have been carried out on the phone to people I have never seen and the results are just as effective. I have rarely encountered a case where the sitters did not immediately identify with any 'lives' presented to them in this way.

The first time I 'linked in' to a previous existence as an animal was at a Psychic Fair held in a large hotel in Earls Court over a

Bank Holiday weekend. Sandy, a rather nondescript young woman, was sitting expectantly holding my hands while I concentrated. I spoke rather cautiously, since I was not sure how she would react to what I had to tell her.

'This life was early on, prehistoric. You lived then but—well, you were not a man or a woman. I seem to be seeing you as some sort of an animal that inhabited the earth at that time. At least I suppose it is the earth, though the whole sky is red, swirling and moving like a kind of gas, as though maybe the sun had not cooled down.'

Sandy prompted: 'Yes?' while I paused to consider the image in my mind.

'Well, you were just one of the creatures that lived then. I don't know what they were, some sort of deer, very gentle and timid. They were vegetarian, they nibbled very delicately on bits of—moss, I think it is. There doesn't seem to have been much vegetation actually, the earth is bare, something like tundra, dark, with these clumps of moss or whatever they are here and there, and the creatures are just grazing quietly while the sky burns.'

Sandy sighed.

'That is exactly how I feel,' she said. 'Gentle and timid, trying to cope while all around me the world is burning. If you had said I was a caveman or something I wouldn't have identified with it at all. I don't have that sort of aggression, that sense of looking out for myself. I can't do it. Yes, I am sure you are right, I was one of the timid creatures. I still am.'

We were able to discuss different kinds of philosophies, different kinds of strengths, how necessary gentleness and timidity are as well as aggression. Sandy gained a great deal of helpful insight into her present circumstances from her life as a prehistoric 'deer creature' (probably long since extinct). But it was rather difficult at first for me to take it for granted that I might encounter further cases of this kind.

As I have detailed in my book on past lives, there can never be any definite proof that we have lived lives before this one. So far as I am aware there has never been a single case where a person has been proved beyond doubt to have existed previously in another body, whether identifiable or not. Even cases filled with factual data and circumstantial evidence are not conclusive since there are many ways in which the human mind can, consciously or unconsciously, provide this sort of evidence— and even more realistically, such evidence is literally impossible to check or verify. So in one sense we have to regard all accounts of past lives and previous existence as hearsay.

But if we are willing to accept theories of reincarnation and past lives on trust, in faith, as we accept the existence of everything else we cannot prove to the satisfaction of our physical senses—including God—it is reasonable to suppose that all the lives which reveal themselves to us are probably equally genuine. I had to take this attitude when I began to encounter cases of past existence as animals, insects, even strange creatures I could hardly describe far less identify, in the course of my work.

I was aware that according to many religions the soul can pass through different lives, learning and progressing as it does so, and that some of these lives might be expected to be of the 'lower orders'—animals or in some cases, even insects or plants. But I had never heard of a serious case where a human sitter had actually been regressed to a life other than that of a human being.

Some of the reasons for this seemed obvious. For instance if a person went back to life as, say, a dog one might imagine it would pose quite a lot of difficulties in communication. Could a dog make an effective comment that could be taken seriously? And how could details be conveyed if the past life was that of a bird or a fish or beetle?

But as with my own regression to life as a cat, there has turned out to be no problem so far as I am concerned. Just as 'channelled' material is absorbed through a kind of mental osmosis rather than being dictated in any sort of language, awareness of all previous lives to which I might 'link in'—whether human, animal or even insect or 'creature'—is similarly communicated.

Unannounced, the animal lives continued to appear during my daily work as a psychic. One woman seemed to have existed briefly as a young bear which I saw being hunted down in the snowy wastes of the Russian steppes by men on horseback. Another who had met a violent end had been a deer killed in the chase. I saw her being torn to pieces by the hounds and felt her anguish.

A very spectacular case was the 'fish-creature' of incredible mental power and arrogance that appeared to have existed in some early civilisation I could not identify. I detailed this case with references to some of the others in my book on past lives, mentioning that though I had felt apologetic about telling my sitter, Angie, that she had been 'a sort of fish creature, made of jelly with trailing fins', corroborative evidence for this unlikely claim actually came to light months after the session. Apparently one early form of life on earth could well have been of the invertebrate type—some kind of fish.

But as well as encountering examples of past lives that human sitters had lived as animals, I found myself receiving messages from the spirits of animals who had died and

117

wanted to communicate with owners they had loved in life and who had loved them. There appeared to be little difference, so far as messages from the spiritual world were concerned, whether the departed had been human or animal. This suggested that some animals at least had individual souls which continued to exist in spirit form after death. Another of my books, *A Psychic's Casebook* gives brief details of some of those early animal messages—from a devoted Cornish Rex cat whose owner had been devastated at his loss; a white mare who was unable to express herself but wanted her previous owner to know that she was there 'to be remembered'; and a recently departed dog whose mistress was mourning his loss very deeply.

Though the spirits of these animals did not pass on specific messages in words their intention was quite clear. They came prompted entirely by love, wanting to reassure their owners and comfort them. More and more animal lives and animal messages were added to the list over a period of years and eventually, since I was not aware of anyone else who had ever conducted any kind of survey based on this sort of information, I decided to try some experiments.

My own experience and the cases I have dealt with involving other people suggest that human and animal existences actually alternate, though for no apparent reason. I considered whether this might happen because, as some religious teachings claim, the way we live each life is a preparation for the next. Brutal behaviour in a human being, therefore, would result in a kind of down-grading to some sort of brutish existence in the next life while an animal, wolf or hyena, say, might earn the right to be a human being the next time round. I found this explanation unsatisfactory in view of the intense, intuitive spiritual quality of the animal lives and communications I have dealt with as well as the capacity of animals to act with complete integrity and purity of motive. Animal lives, whatever else they might be, are not some kind of punishment for bad behaviour in human beings.

Since I had come across many examples of human sitters who had experienced animal as well as human existence in the past I wondered whether this indicated that some animals too might have experienced both kinds of lives. Since I can 'link in' to past lives effectively for human sitters simply by concentrating my mental energy, I wondered whether it was possible I could use the same method to regress animals and 'link in' to previous lives they might have experienced as human beings.

It seemed extremely far-fetched and I had no idea at all what to expect, if anything, but I set about opening a casebook of animal regressions, working with an entirely open mind and in as realistic a manner as possible. I 'linked in', concentrating on each animal in exactly the same manner as I worked with human sitters. Then immediately afterwards I recorded exactly what the result had been.

I tested 'linking in' first on my pet miniature dove as he sat in his cage in the conservatory and entered up the following 'case notes' for my little bird:

CASE 1: GLORY (Glo). Diamond dove age 5 years.

Previous history: Survived the loss of his mate at 1 year and various adjustments to new cages and their positions, company of other birds and a recent long journey by van to a new home.

Characteristic behaviour: Extremely placid and loving.

PAST LIFE IMPRESSIONS

The only picture that seemed to come when I regressed Glo by concentrating and holding him in my mind while I linked in with his past, was a vague swirl of silver like the mist of a far constellation in deep space, more sensed than real. No emotion, no sense of a 'life' as such. But other impressions did occur:

'He did not ask me to regress him, and it makes no difference to him what I find/do not find. He is completely unaware.

'A sensation of being only, any 'personality' has been superimposed. He seems to be organic only, programmed to respond.

'The silver mist seems a sort of corporate soul, pure energy. He (Glo) embodies universal innocence and purity, but his "soul" as an individual is projected—(by me? By his present 'incarnation?)'

By this time I had left London and was living in the Midlands. Intrigued by the result of Glo's regression session, I made a visit to Trentham Gardens (a local tourist attraction) that afternoon hoping to 'regress' a wider selection of animal subjects. It had become immediately obvious that behavioural or other details I had intended to include as part of my case notes would hardly ever be available but as I never asked for such details from human sitters I felt this would not matter.

It was raining heavily and the small zoo was closed but standing at the lakeside I made a further test, 'linking in' for:

CASE 2: UNNAMED GOOSE (DRAKE).

The drake was standing with some ducks who were feeding. Immediately after I had conducted his regression, I noted the results down over a cup of coffee in the café:

'Instant picture like a snapshot, a film 'still', extremely clear, of a mediaeval market, out of doors. I saw a woman, very plump and buxom with dark hair curling loose on her shoulders. Aged about 30, height about 4 feet 11 inches. She was wearing some sort of long dark brown garment, like sacking, pulled in tight round her waist, and she was laughing, her mouth open, red lips and sparkly dark eyes. Might have been Welsh. She was selling something, a sort of peasant type.'

CASE 3: UNNAMED MUTE SWAN

Further along the lake I regressed one individual from a group of swans while observing it (I did not know whether it was male or female) through the wide meshes of a wire fence.

'There does not seem to be anything only a kind of vacuum, a bit like the deep space in Glo's regression. I get the feeling that the swan is very empty-headed for all its beauty, it has no mind or individual "soul", seems to be only energy from the same sort of corporate soul. No pictures of a past of any sort that I can recognise or identify.'

In all my experience of regressions I had come across only one or two cases where birds were present and none of these had really seemed to make much sense. The images from these three bird regressions intensified my conviction that the lower order of such creatures probably existed as spontaneous 'sparks from the soul of God' without a fully

122

developed identity. The pictures I received from Glo and the swan indicated that there was no real memory of a finite existence, only of something very vague.

But what about the drake and the vision of a woman laughing in a mediaeval market? This very clear, though unexpected image opened up new possibilities but I made no effort to theorise. I pursued my case histories, moving on to what are generally regarded as higher life forms than birds. If a drake could have existed as a human being, the chances seemed more than likely that a dog or cat had probably done so too.

CASE 4: TARA (TORTOISESHELL PERSIAN CAT)

I had known Tara (15 years old) for some time as the pet of neighbours when I had lived in London. I planned to regress her when I visited London on business, but while arranging matters on the phone I was consciously 'holding' her in my mind while talking to her owner and I found an image came through very clearly even though I was over a hundred miles away. I have said I perform similar link ups to past lives for human clients during phone consultations.

This time, though, I was not prepared to accept what I had seen until I was actually with Tara herself in South-west London. When I carried out her regression in my former

123

neighbours' flat, however, the original picture did not change but was strengthened and intensified. This is the report I made:

'While speaking on the phone I saw very clearly the outline of a nun's head and long robe, in black with a white coif such as nuns have round their face. I knew Tara had been a Mother Superior, somewhere very isolated, on a sea coast. The name Tara is very Irish and I am a little suspicious of this next bit, but I got the impression that the place was on the Atlantic coast of Ireland, somewhere in the north-west.

'When I concentrated on "linking in" while in the room with Tara, I had an even deeper impression of a wild coastline, high winds, cliffs and tempestuous waves. I saw also stone walls and a stone-flagged corridor, very bare, with arched windows opening out along it, though there was no glass in them. It was very lonely, very cold and damp. Tara lived there a long time and she must have been an abbess because they called her "Mother".'

In fact Tara had suffered for some years from stiffness in the joints of her legs and paws. I felt she had carried this with her into the present from the intense damp and cold of her life of privation as a nun.

CASE 5: JAKE (BLUE ROAN COCKER SPANIEL)

Jake was another pet of my former London

neighbours, 4 years old and as they described him fondly: 'A real silly.' When I concentrated on 'holding' him in my mind to regress him I received the following image:

'I can see very clearly a floor, with rushes on it, and there is a cradle standing in the room, about three feet high, on legs. I can't see the baby in the cradle, but it was a boy and he was born to a high estate. The time is about 1400, I have a vague glimpse of the sort of clothes they wore, short tunics and long hose. It was in France, in one of the little kingdoms there were then or a dukedom or something like that. The baby was a prince or the heir to a dukedom or a county. I see him as a very young baby, but in front of him there were looming the burdens he would have to carry because of his high birth. I feel that it would not have been an enviable destiny.'

CASE 6: TIKI (CHOCOLATE POINT SIAMESE)
and
CASE 7: TIA (SEAL POINT SIAMESE)

I regressed the two eight month old cats in turn as they slept curled up together in their basket after playing. For Tiki, the slightly larger male, this was the image I received:

'There are birds circling a lighthouse or tower on the coast of a sea in the southern hemisphere, the Mediterranean I think. They are whitish—a sort of grey off-white really,

125

seabirds, I suppose. The lighthouse—well, it can't be a lighthouse because it is too narrow, but it is like a tower, tall into the sky—.'

'A minaret?' was the suggestion put forward simultaneously by both the cats' owner and my friend Paul, who were listening.

I considered.

'Yes, I suppose it is a minaret—but the mind of whoever or whatever is looking at the scene, Tiki's past self, does not know it is a minaret.' I had of course come across the same thing in my own regression to past life as a cat. I had been able to say afterwards that 'I went into the street' but at the time, the animal mind within which I was viewing the scene did not know what a street was. Human terms mean nothing to an animal.

I could get no other details for Tiki sensation of delicate blue Mediterranean sky and light and birds continuing to circle. I assumed he must have existed previously as one of the birds since I could not connect with any other creature.

For Tia the little female, there was a very different image:

'A young girl of about fourteen or fifteen, sitting on a litter being carried to some kind of celebration, probably her wedding. She is dark haired and very lovely. The litter is open and I can see her through the side but she is draped all over, including her head, with a sort of open-weave silver shawl or gauze of some sort

126

with silver coins sewn in so that they move very softly and shine. I think it is in Persia, a long time ago. I can sense pink roses nearby. She is just like a little spoiled kitten, sensuous and delicate under all that silver.'

CASE 8: UNKNOWN MAGPIE

Looking out of the window while having breakfast, watching birds feeding on the lawn, I 'held' one of the magpies in my mind as a random experiment to see what I obtained. In a fast sensation of rushing down a tunnel mentally, I emerged to be aware of:

'A stone city or brick, but eastern, something like the Middle East. The buildings are half-fallen in and it is very ruinous and poor. There seem to be people wandering about in terrible squalor. I think the magpie was one of these people. I can't tell the date, it is very vague. I am only really seeing the stones fallen in heaps.'

In the majority of cases of animal regression, the image I received was a kind of snapshot, a still picture of arrested motion lacking the emotional depth that generally accompanies the regressions of human sitters—though in some of the animal cases the emotional depth was stronger than others. Occasionally there seemed to be a sort of 'race memory' awareness but sometimes (as with my little dove Glo), there was not even that. Nothing emerged except an impression of swirling mist or space, as though the creature had come straight from an existence as pure energy without shape or form.

During a second visit I made to the small zoo at Trentham Gardens, I was able to regress some more exotic subjects.

CASE 9: GREEN IGUANA (MALE)
and
CASE 10: SMALLER GREEN IGUANA (FEMALE?)

These were regressed together since they occupied the same reptile tank, appearing to drowse in the hot concentrated light. I 'held' the larger male in my mind first, reporting afterwards:

'The impressions are confused. I seemed to get a fleeting glimpse of a great Emperor, parchment-like and wrinkled with age, in ancient Japan, I think. But as soon as it came it was gone and there was a landscape seen from above, very soft and misty green. I envisaged this as somewhere in the Scottish islands. Nothing really definite though, just a great deal of confusion and vague images.'

In contrast a clear picture came through immediately when I regressed the smaller iguana.

'A child about four or so, a toddler, holding a red balloon on a long string. It is at a fair, a funfair in Europe some time in the 20th century. There are crowds of people and a lot of noise (I can't hear it but I am aware of it), lights flashing and colours, but as with the woman laughing in the mediaeval market, only the image of the child holding the balloon seems to stand out.'

CASE 11: BURMESE PYTHON (FEMALE)

'I see a wise man, a prophet beside the Ganges. He is sitting by the river meditating. He is small and thin, with round wire-type spectacles and a sort of hat flattened on top. He is old. The name of Gandhi is very strong. He is looking at me as though to say: "I know what you are thinking. You don't believe this, do you?" It is true, I find it difficult to take but it is very clear. I can see the waters flowing and there seem to be mountains or hills in the distance, but there is nothing else except him.'

CASE 12: WHITE DONKEY
and
CASE 13: RETIRED PIT PONY

Two donkeys and a retired pit pony were enjoying the sun as they shared the same field. I concentrated first on one of the donkeys.

'I get the colour yellow. It is a yellow room, the walls all silk, I think, and the donkey was the girl who sat in it, a courtesan maybe, in ancient Japan. I can see her toenails, long and painted. They are the clearest detail to come through, very very long. She sat there in the yellow room and hardly ever moved. She was a concubine not a courtesan, I think, more important, somebody very important, but she seems languid and as though the yellow room was a prison. I don't think she ever went out. The yellow room has a low ceiling. It's quite tiny, but very rich and opulent—the yellow colour is very clear.'

The pit pony's regression produced the following:

'This is a simple picture, a girl on a seashore with long dark hair, about fifteen, Greek I think. That is all I see, just the long hair and the sea and part of a little boat. She has her back to me, turning, holding onto the side of the boat as it rests on the sand. An impression of light and air all around.'

CASE 13: COMMON BUZZARD

I concentrated on this magnificent bird of prey as it sat motionless in its wire enclosure.

'I seem to be high above the landscape, looking down on what I think is Hadrian's Wall winding across the green land below. This is from the viewpoint I might have expected if a dead soul was just passing from the body, but I do not think it is a soul passing, more a generality, as though it was a memory glimpse, perhaps glimpsed in a past life as another bird. It is difficult to gather any information. The scene is just there, empty.'

130

Rather rough and ready it may be but I hope my 'Animal Regression Casebook' is no less interesting for that. I leave readers to decide for themselves what conclusions—if any—they want to draw from the examples I have given above.

My own feeling as I carried out my regressions with animal subjects was that the whole popular concept of human existence as superior to that of animals was being challenged, enlarged and widened to encompass wonderful possibilities. Human or animal, these are surely all spiritual equals through which souls may continue to pass as each becomes relevant.

One past life session I conducted on the phone for a lady called Tina (described in my book on past lives) revealed several previous lives involving animals, some dark and painful. In this case Tina had not, of course, actually regressed in trance herself but after the book was published she sent me the following poem describing what awareness of her past lives both human and animal had meant to her. It is reproduced here with her permission.

JOURNEYS THROUGH THE PAST

Stone slabs on floor,
smell of roasting, as a spit
rotates over flames; stock
bubbling in a huge Elizabethan kitchen,
where high windows let in daylight
but allow no distracting view.
A cat sits warm, contented,
satisfied everything is in order,
no one else is here, he is in charge,
this is his domain.

I am the cat.

Small child with dark curly hair
bare feet, grass skirt,
laughing, splashes in river, runs
to yellow flowers on banks. Happy.
From a thousand years ago,
her life is simple, peaceful, good.

I am the girl.

Forward now to more recent time
to a Portuguese fishing village:
where a lad struggles with nets
from his father's boat,
mending holes.

I am that boy.

Hearing screams in her head
from animals in gin traps,
a young girl, lying awake
in country dark, writhes with their pain,
knows she is helpless
can do nothing for them
weeps in sympathy.

I am that girl.

Today's adult, attempting
to keep the innocence
of the cat and the children,
their intuition and wisdom,
walks among nets.

Thus the psychic spoke.

Belief or disbelief
is unimportant, I have no memory
of those lives, those children.
But they are still strong within
must teach me how to undo knots
dodge traps, reclaim harmony.

Some of the words Tina has used in this poem
occur time and time again when one
encounters attempts to describe past lives
experienced as animals: harmony, innocence,
intuitive wisdom.
They may seem sentimental or even naïve

when we try to relate them to today's tough way of living but these are powerful strengths which animals possess, and which we can share when we return to those past existences in animal form. And there are others: most notably, love.

I met Emma at a Psychic Fair where we were both working, myself as a psychic and Emma selling books, gem stones, jewellery and other items. I learned that she ran a New Age shop and healing centre in Greenwich and we became friends. She and her partner Joe were two very tough, street-wise people—Joe had drifted in the rock music scene experimenting with sex and drugs before they found each other spiritually as well as physically in this life. They were convinced they shared a chequered past and felt their mutual history had been long and at times blissfully happy, yet filled with unbearable shadows of separation and loss.

Hearing that I was writing about past lives particularly those involving animals, they described to me their own experience of a shared meditation where they had jointly regressed to life together as whales. This was of particular interest since apart from my own regression to awareness of being a cat, most of the other cases I had encountered did not involve actual physical regression while in trance—though my book on past lives did

134

include one account of apparent life as a spider.

This was how Emma and Joe described their experience:

JOE: I'm looking down through a blanket of stars. There's a moonlit sea shimmering down before me. I start to move very quickly through a tunnel and then there's this flash of white light. I become conscious of my surroundings and notice I'm below the ocean, moving very slowly.

EMMA: I find myself floating in the depths of space. I notice the earth is in darkness and there is only sea. I become aware that there is another energy or being at the side of me. I suddenly hear the sounds of whales echoing all around, and then within seconds I am in the body of a whale, moving silently through the water.

BOTH: We feel we are moving along in harmony, a very peaceful feeling. It's almost a knowing feeling, that we are part of the universe, everything is in order. There is also an immense feeling of love.

EMMA: I am feeling drawn to the whale beside me. It's like a magnet, I remember seeing a flash of pink at the side of me.

JOE: I became responsive to the energy beside me, then I had this amazing feeling. There was a rush of energy followed by stillness. It seemed to be over in a matter of minutes.

At this point their shared meditation ended but both felt it was important to return to that past life and they continued it at a later date.

Emma reported:

EMMA: As I tried to go back I found that my physical body began to ache and my stomach felt like it was having contractions. I went a bit dizzy and then slipped back into that life. I remember pain, and then looking down and seeing a baby whale, and then I was moving slowly along with the other whale at my side. I also remember being able to see above the water and noticed a coastline, and somehow knew that we were heading towards it.

JOE: I am aware of moving alongside the other whale, and I feel very protective towards it, like I have a duty. I also know that something has changed or the circumstances are now different. It's weird to think that an animal can have that kind of instinctive knowing.

This account in its simplicity and gentleness (all the more moving, I feel, since it is given by two very tough people) seems to contain the wonder and miracle of the birth of a baby whale in as authentic a manner as if whales themselves had spoken to us, whether one actually accepts it as a personal experience or not.

It is noticeable (as we have already seen in

my own recollection of being a cat and in Tina's poem) that in trying to describe past lives as animals the language becomes charged with emotions that are difficult to capture in ordinary everyday speech. Such experiences are almost mystical. They are suffused with an awareness of the divine, particularly in its caring and reassuring aspects, an overwhelming sensation of the rightness of existence, of being, of everything; and the consciousness of great peace. Even in the cases where I have 'linked in' to such lives and described them to sitters, there seems to have been some sort of transmuted mystical gift that has helped the people concerned to be able to accept reality for what it is and to find tranquillity.

My researches in this field have been very basic and are incomplete but I think every human being intuitively knows that animals have a great deal to give and to teach our apparently superior species. They carry with them the love of God (for want of a better phrase), they know God in their own simple, intuitive way which is positivity itself. This is embodied in the manner in which they live their lives, unselfconsciously, free from the human concepts of guilt, shame and sin and the selfishness of the ego.

The fact that they often have to carry also the angers, frustrations, arrogance and dark cruel impulses of the human psyche, and that they accept this with the same humility of a spirit at peace with itself, suggests to me that perhaps it is the animals—or some of them, at any rate—who may be the superior souls. I cannot help recalling that cryptic reminder in the Bible about 'entertaining angels unawares.'

CHAPTER SEVEN

COMING TO TERMS: CASE HISTORIES

Though I have never made any claim to be
more competent or 'advanced' than anyone
else I have found that since I first began
practising as a psychic, the people who are
prompted to consult me are often highly gifted
psychically themselves. Sometimes they are
extremely spiritually advanced and at one time
I wondered why such people needed to consult
anyone at all, let alone why they thought I
could help or advise them.

I came to accept, though, that everyone has
some particular role to fulfil, all equally
necessary and relevant. Even the wise and the
strong sometimes need encouragement and as
I think my own story illustrates, it is often not
easy to accept the way forward particularly if
this involves adjusting to the fact that one
possesses insight or ability which seems to
mark one out as 'odd', different to other
people.

The case histories in this next chapter
highlight some of the problems I encounter
again and again in various forms—and the fact
that the individuals mentioned are all female
does not mean that only women can have
difficulty with their psychic progress. But a

very large percentage of the people who consult me happen to be women and these cases are particularly representative.

Marilyn: Life, But Which One?

It is always sad when someone seems chronically unable to come to terms with life. Breakdowns, psychiatric treatment, even drugs to help the individual cope become a part of everyday existence both for the sufferer and for his/her family.

There is a sense of inadequacy and failure, a conviction that one is less competent or brave than everyone else. The sufferers feel hurtfully aware that even the seemingly basic traumas of living appear to be beyond them and may become convinced that however hard they try they will never be anything other than second-rate, a burden to hardy souls who can apparently relate to 'real life' in the 'real world' without cracking up.

In many cases—though of course not all—seemingly miraculous cures can be effected when sufferers stop feverishly trying to come to terms with what everyone else tells them is 'real life' and 'reality' and are encouraged to examine what 'reality' actually means to them—something they may never have been allowed, or allowed themselves, to do before.

Very psychic people who 'see' things or even more subtly perceive and think things which are not of the way of this world can be led to cripple themselves mentally, and taught to doubt their own senses. They may grow up unable to trust even the evidence of their own life experience, their own judgement about what they 'see', what is really 'real' to them. The 'reality' to which they so desperately and hopelessly aspire in these cases has been imposed on them (often in the most well-meaning way) by concerned relatives or friends. The sufferer can spend a lifetime trying to come to terms with a world in which he or she quite literally does not belong and which is, to him or her, as unreal as a two-dimensional picture book.

Marilyn was passing through a traumatic spiritual crisis when I saw her. She was an intelligent, alert woman in her early forties who in spite of having suffered breakdown after breakdown had managed to make a career for herself as a commercial artist. She was perhaps too educated about what she saw as her psychological deficiencies to be able to view herself objectively.

Her husband and two grown-up children had been unfailingly supportive and tried to reassure her that she was loved and valued as a person but she knew that even they did not really understand what her problem was.

'I am helpless, like a prisoner. I feel literally unable to move or do anything without permission, powerless, you know?' she explained and I was struck by the depth of angry frustration seething beneath her words. Ashamed to express her feelings against her family, those around her who were trying their best to help and thinking they were giving her the assistance she needed, she had no outlet for her frustrated fury. All her life she had turned it inwards onto herself, making herself ill.

'It has always been like this,' she continued after a moment. 'I don't ever remember being any different. I have never been able to cope—only for short periods, then somehow I'd go off the rails—.'

'In what way? You are a very strong-willed person. You are quite competent to make decisions even if the things you choose to do and the ways you want to go are not what other people might choose. You're just different—or rather, they are different from *you*,' I encouraged.

She shook her head with gloomy finality.

'No, I dare not make choices, or do anything. I am always wrong, you see.'

'How do you know that?'

She stared.

'Well—if everyone else is right, then I must be wrong, mustn't I?'

'About what in particular?' I asked, and she shrugged in increasing irritation at my obtuseness.

'About everything. Life. The way things are.'

'Marilyn,' I said carefully. 'I want you just for a moment, just for one moment, to look at it the other way round. What if it's you who've been right all the time, even though everyone else told you you were wrong, that things couldn't be the way you thought, and happen the way you said they did?'

'You mean—.' She groped for words. 'They are wrong, then?'

'No,' I suggested gently. 'They are right too, but in a different kind of way, a way that's right for them.'

It took Marilyn some time to adjust to the possibility that the world she had tried so hard to deny, the world of her own inhabiting where the physical and the spiritual overlapped, might actually be acceptable to others. To realise that there were other people like herself, people who were 'sighted', and who also found 'their' world more real to them than any imposed external reality.

The sudden reversal, the sudden shift in perception, at first confused and frightened her but once she was able to find her feet in the world where she belonged, she lost her helplessness and frustration. It was a joy to see her soar mentally, with the confidence of a bird let loose from a cage into its own element. A few years later when we met again, she was using her spiritual and psychic resources as well as her artistic training, working with handicapped students who were unable to paint or draw with their hands, helping them to 'see' beyond the physical world into realities beyond.

Joanne: On Her Own Terms

But it is not enough just to be prepared to remove confining boundaries and accept a wider vision of existence. Over-enthusiastic, undisciplined wallowing—even in an awareness of the psychic—can be just as negative as dismissing it out of hand.

Joanne was another very strong-willed woman. In fact it is the strong-willed and determined who often run into trouble over the acceptance of their abilities or powers since they refuse to let themselves be taken by the spiritual current, as it were, and insist on trying to swim against the tide.

In spite of her strong personality Joanne had apparently chosen a submissive role in her marriage, though she did not respect her husband. Even while claiming to subordinate herself to his wishes and interests she secretly considered she deserved better from life, and when after the birth of her daughter she discovered she possessed extremely powerful clairvoyant vision, she seized on this as an excuse to abandon her previously down-trodden role.

She proceeded to surround herself with

mystical drama. A somewhat dull, stolid personality—actually heavy-set and rather overweight in physical build—she re-invented herself as the most melodramatic type of 'stage medium'. She never stopped playing her role. She would sweep into rooms only to pause on the threshold declaring that she was 'picking up' spirits everywhere, that they were passing through her in throbbing waves of energy, sometimes causing her actual physical discomfort, even pain.

'But I can stand it,' she assured concerned witnesses with a martyred smile, proceeding on her self-appointed course. She spent a good deal of her time in church, witnessing the spirits of the dead rising at funeral services and feeling them pass through her, scattering crystals of purity as they ascended to heaven. She could not refrain from pointing out to all and sundry how ghosts and spirits swarmed about them, urging them to change this terrible world, in its blindness and callousness, into a place of shining light.

She told me, in increasing distress when she consulted me, that the wickedness and evil that pervaded the world was unbearable to her now that her clairvoyant vision allowed her to see terrible things everywhere.

'When I walk down the street I can see lewd thoughts in people's heads. I can see people in bars touching each other—you know what I mean—and writhing naked on the floor. I see images everywhere—.' Her voice sank to a shaking whisper. 'Images of—well, genitals—. The world is so wicked, so terrible.'

Joanne had been persuaded to consult a psychiatrist. In fact she had seen two and both had assured her that she was utterly sane. But her husband, unable to cope with her outpouring of visionary truths, had plunged into an affair with a younger woman and Joanne was quietly distraught when she came to me.

'What is the matter with me?' she asked and there was no doubting her complete sincerity. 'Is it me? I know I see the truth, I don't care what the rest of the world thinks. I would die for the truth. I would be glad to go anyway, this world is such a ghastly place.'

I told her I agreed with the psychiatrists, that I thought she was quite sane. But in a way this made it even more difficult for her.

'You need to learn to discipline yourself,' I suggested. 'There is no doubt that you have an amazing psychic gift. But if you just let yourself be hit by every single image or ghostly or spiritual energy that throws itself at you, however truthful it is, without making any attempt to protect yourself or control your vision, you might quite literally be bombarded beyond endurance.'

She waved a dismissive hand, assuring me:

'I have been close to death several times. When the energies passed through, sometimes

146

they were awful—it was agonising and I don't know how I survived. But I did. It's amazing, you know, what the body can stand, and the mind as well.'

I suggested that perhaps it was not necessary for her to involve herself so uncompromisingly in the activities of spiritual energies. Nor was there any need for her to torment herself with the sexual images that she found so distressing.

'You think I am doing it to myself? That I am responsible for it all?' she asked incredulously.

'You have never come to terms with your own sexuality,' I told her. 'You identify your sexual urges with sin or shame or guilt and as often happens with this kind of syndrome, you also desperately need to feel in control, and find it difficult to "let go". On the higher levels, dealing with spiritual things, you are comfortable even if you are pushing yourself to the physical limits, but you do not want, or feel able, to cope with your own physical self. And because this is your weakest point this is where any trouble caused by a lack of balance in your personality will make itself manifest.'

In fact Joanne had seized on her awareness of psychic power as a defence behind which she tried to hide from the areas of physical living she did not want to acknowledge. Until she accepted not only the fact that she was extremely clairvoyant but also that she was a human being with a life to live in the physical present, I thought she would continue to experience the disturbing visions which caused her such distress.

'If you are going to be able to employ your gifts usefully, you need to be able to see the world—and the evils within it as well as the wonders—without judging it, completely dispassionately,' I told her. 'It is all there for a reason, even if you think otherwise.'

She went away unconvinced, her powerful ego reluctant to 'let go' even to a higher power. I have come across many other cases like this where psychic or even mystical insight is accepted seemingly whole-heartedly and the individual concerned appears completely dedicated. But in such situations there is nearly always, however well hidden, some form of concealed agenda.

Joanne was only too eager to be a 'power for the spirit', there for others even if she had to suffer personally in the process—but so long as she could do it her own way. She did not want to know about the spiritual discipline that was required, or tackle the unresolved conflicts within herself.

Donna: The Answer She Wanted

I have already mentioned that most people intuitively know which way they should go when there is any decision to be made regarding their spiritual development or life progress. They may not want to recognise the truth or face it, but they are aware of it all the same.

Sitters rarely tell me that I have revealed new or unexpected information to them after a consultation. Rather, what I (along with most other consultants in this field) am told is that: 'You have reassured me about what I already knew I had to do' or 'You have helped me to see clearly what I really knew all along, deep down.'

In most cases it is not the actual action to be taken or the way to be followed, however difficult or daunting these may be, which poses the problem. Neither is it usually any lack of courage or moral fibre. Generally the way forward for the person with the problem would actually be easier for them than the alternative.

But having most earnestly requested help, advice, guidance, sometimes even specific instructions, some individuals who have asked for answers—while acknowledging that the answers they have been given are the ones they needed—then proceed to shy away from them, excuse themselves from acting on them and reject them. Not only that but they will follow the same procedure time after time, with one mentor after another.

Donna, a strong-willed, erudite woman of

great potential was in her mid-twenties. She had been treated in many clinics over a period of ten years for an unspecified problem that had completely incapacitated her and prevented her from living any sort of meaningful life at all. She had never been able to work, and had several times attempted suicide. Her existence was ruled by obsessive behavioural rituals, and she became angry when one of the psychiatrists she consulted told her that though she claimed to be depressed, she was not actually suffering from a clinical depressive illness.

She told me she had felt so strongly about this apparent minimising of her situation that she had gone to waylay the woman, intending to 'strangle her' when she left her office. In the event the woman did not emerge, and in her frustration Donna had walked deliberately in front of a car in London's rush hour traffic, causing herself injury instead.

When I saw her, I told her that in my opinion there was little wrong with her that she could not put right by letting go her anger and her resistance and accepting her life, her potential and the building of her future positively. I thought the psychiatrist was right and she was not mentally ill. Instead, she was more than averagely gifted. But Donna was not pleased in spite of her insistence that she desperately wanted to be 'normal' and 'get better'.

'You are never going to be "normal" in the sense that the average person is "normal". You have talents and abilities that will mean you are always going to be marked as different, in the way that geniuses and other highly intuitive people are,' I told her bluntly. 'It is this that you do not want to accept. There is a responsibility that comes with the gift of vision. And it is this responsibility you are trying to reject, by turning your "apartness" and "difference" into something weak and negative that will get you sympathy, rather than working at earning respect for being what you really are. You're trying to evade the issue in all ways you can, trying to pretend it isn't there, that the issue is something else altogether.'

Donna replied curtly that she was disappointed with what I had said since 'You are supposed to be very good, and I really thought you would be able to help me.' She had come some hundred miles to see me in person, insisting on making the journey, but she departed frostily, mentioning the name of another practitioner she had heard of (in America, this time) who, she was now convinced, was the only one who would be able to provide the miracle cure she needed.

I have seen this syndrome many times. Anyone with experience of such cases (whether they are psychic or not) will know that the sufferer will go in frustration and increasing anger from one authority to the other, never actually finding the 'advice' they claim to be seeking nor the miracle they are convinced will free them from their terrible bondage.

'Just give me peace, that is all I ask,' they cry. But until they are willing to accept the responsibility for themselves and their own lives rather than going through the motions of consulting others in the hope that someone will actually give them permission to avoid tackling their problems constructively, they will never be able to find that peace is something within themselves, not something imposed. And they will never be truly free, though the chains are of entirely their own making.

Rita and Enid: Sacrificial Lambs

Often there is a refusal to accept the potential of the gifts one has been given, apparently for the most worthy of reasons. It is very difficult to understand that 'doing good' or 'doing the right thing' may not, sometimes, be such an entirely praiseworthy course of action as it seems.

Rita, a lady in her seventies, had been a singer but on her marriage had given up her career to devote herself to her husband's interests. Now, much later in life, she was caring single-handedly for her husband after he had suffered a series of strokes. He was enfeebled, vague, incontinent and inclined to keep her awake at all hours of the night.

Rita had been looking after her husband in this manner for nearly ten years—as his chauffeur, nurse, companion, cook, coping with his heavy laundry—disregarding the fact that she suffered from quite serious and debilitating health problems herself. When she had a sitting with me, the first thing I saw was that her situation could have been dramatically eased immediately, if only she had made a slight effort to alter it.

Money was not—in this case—a problem so she could have hired even part-time assistance to relieve her of her burden of responsibility and household toiling. In fact the whole situation could very easily have been organised far more efficiently so that both she and her husband would have benefited.

I pointed these things out to her. She said she agreed with me—but that was as far as it went. The situation remained the same. But later Rita had a regression session with me. She was a very strong personality, for all that she had chosen a passive role in her marriage, and I was not surprised that the previous life which I 'linked into' for her was extremely powerful.

'A sense of gloom, pain, a dark place, a dungeon or torture chamber deep underground down a long flight of stone steps. They are roughly hewn, damp where water is dripping. I think you lived here—or existed would be a better word,' I told her. 'You were a man then but crippled and deformed, the body very twisted. I think you were dumb—maybe deaf as well. You slept on the floor of this place, huddled in a corner. The rest of the time you assisted in a menial kind of way with the activities in the chambers where people were being held and tortured—though you took no part in any of the torture yourself. I think you were limited intellectually as well as physically and had no real understanding of what was going on.'

The time seemed to have been vaguely 15th Century but it was impossible to know the place or country since there was no awareness of any outside world. The whole horizon of this previous life of Rita's was enclosed within the dungeon walls.

'You were a throw-out from society,' I said. 'You had just been pushed there and left there to become a part of the dungeon, but you were quite fond of it in a strange way, I think. It was all you were familiar with, all you knew.'

Rita identified rather glumly with this previous life since, as we both agreed, her present existence was similarly restricted and she had no personal freedom. When I examined her past lives further I found there seemed to be nothing else but more dark, more helplessness and confinement.

'And yet,' I told her, considering, 'you were not a prisoner yourself. You could have gone out of the dungeon, climbed the steps and found the doorway that led out into the courtyard.'

I asked her to visualise her past self, crippled and limited, actually making its way up the dark stairs from the dungeon to where the doorway stood open to the sky and the light.

'You are standing with all that open space before you. There is a world out there and you can walk out of the dark into it, just like that, if only you choose. What do you feel at the prospect?'

One might imagine that the idea of being freed, of being let loose from a life of grinding servitude in a dark and painful world would have been seized with relief. I was not surprised, though, when Rita revealed that the concept of all that freedom filled her with fear.

'It is exactly how you are feeling and behaving in this life,' I said. 'You have confined yourself within yet another prison, you live with suffering and despair and you are unable to free yourself, to walk out—not literally but symbolically, by making your own life easier—into some sort of brightness and a fuller existence of your own.'

Rita shook her head, distressed. She was intelligent and realistic and she told me she accepted my comments even though they cut at the very foundations on which she had based her way of life.

'I know you are right. I should think of myself more, and my own needs—I can see that I should care more for myself. But how can I possibly think of myself just now? I have to consider Jack, he must come first. Perhaps,' she added rather wistfully, 'I will be able to try and sort out about myself later on. There is no time while Jack needs me so badly.'

Enid, a fashion shop assistant in her late fifties, put the case to me far more strongly. She had the same problem as Rita, though the circumstances were different since Enid was very aware of her psychic gifts. She said she wanted more than anything to have the time, energy and personal freedom to be able to develop them and progress along the path she felt she needed to follow to find her own fulfilment.

She did not believe in regression or past lives, she told me. She was tougher than Rita, more street-wise, but even so, when I asked why she could not simply make a decision to pursue her spiritual/psychic studies more fully she told me catagorically that it was quite impossible.

'I have to work full-time. It's a question of money, I'm divorced and on my own. I am still paying off my mortgage and trying to get some sort of security for the future. And I have my mother living with me. She is over eighty and ailing. She gets very bitter and dwells on the past a lot and it seems to be always all the things that went wrong, or that she missed out on. I do find it depresses me, I must admit, but she won't take any notice when I try to jolly her up, she is determined only to see the negative side of life, which makes it rather a trial for me. She won't go out or mix with other people though, so she has no-one else to talk to.'

Enid further revealed that her daughter, who lived only a few doors away, had constant problems with her boyfriend. He was in and out of trouble with the police and sometimes violent to her.

'I have to be there for Cindy as well, she never knows what's going to happen next—and of course there is my little grand-daughter, whom I absolutely adore. I have her with me a good deal when I'm not working. No, I have no time at all for myself really, just now. Perhaps when things are more settled in the future—.'

At some stage in every person's spiritual progress, he will have to face up to the fact that he must make a conscious decision about whether his own needs, values and beliefs are more—or less—important to him than the approval of society or the reassuring

157

conviction that he is 'doing his duty' and fulfilling his responsibilities and obligations to those around him. Suggestions that he spare time and energy for himself might well be met with a frown and the freezing response that surely that would be rather selfish.

But as I pointed out to both Rita and Enid, there is never going to be any 'right moment' in the future when everything falls neatly into place and there is time to spare. Each individual must create his own 'right moment'.

As for being selfish, there is all the difference in the world between existing vicariously by courtesy of the needs, demands and even the approval of others, and being freely alive and centred within yourself, making your own decisions and taking full responsibility for them. Nobody was suggesting that Rita or Enid abandon their relatives or leave them to fend for themselves, simply to try a shift in attitude. In an amazingly large number of cases, what seems like selfishness —actually just a consideration that each individual should matter as much to himself as does his partner, parent or child, and that each is just as deserving of his own respect, care and love—would achieve a remarkable transformation.

Quite often, sacrificial individuals are being the opposite of selfless. They may in fact be manipulative and domineering. 'Knowing what is best for her' or 'Being there because he could not manage without me' are actually arrogantly selfish attitudes that can hinder the necessary struggle and progress of others. And they certainly require that those concerned try to examine their own motives more honestly.

Claire: A Burden of Guilt

Those who accept their spiritual or psychic 'sight', and attempt seriously to live by it, can run into problems that can make them feel extremely out of place in an ordered, accepted society. They can never again plead ignorance, never turn from the truth, never delude themselves. And they can never indulge themselves by allowing themselves to behave or react childishly if they are on their way to achieving some degree—however fragmented—of spiritual maturity.

But surely, we might imagine, this is what we are all aiming for in our lives. These qualities of enlightenment, honesty, wisdom— aren't they what we all want to achieve? Aren't they the qualities we admire so much in others, the ones that make us wish we could be like them? Let us hear what Claire, a thirty-eight-year-old who has been working to come to terms with her psychic insight for most of her life, told me as we discussed her situation.

'I am afraid I am just not acceptable to a lot of people,' she said, shrugging. 'They may like me, even love me but they do not love or like the part of me that is trying to live by what I see with my "sight" and must act on. I am beginning to understand that now, though I spent years in confusion and hurt because I could not understand it in the past—and I am afraid many other people can't understand it at all.

'It sounds like arrogance to say this, but while I can empathise with them and make allowances for their limited understanding, they have no capability to understand me on my own level. It's not surprising, really. Anyone who has progressed in any sphere of learning or development can recognise what it is like for those who are just beginning to feel their way, but the "beginners", obviously, can have no conception of what it is like to have advanced further than they have.' She added quietly, 'Often, no tolerance either.'

As we saw in the cases of Rita and Enid the personal quest will, sooner or later, probably clash with the expectations of ordered society. Choices will have to be made that will not be easy because the values are so different.

All spiritual teachings contain this same paradox. In the Bible for instance, Jesus said cryptically that people must 'Give away all you have', and advised his listeners to 'Let the dead bury their dead.' When told his mother and brothers were looking for him, he turned away in an apparently hurtful manner, saying: 'Who are my mother and brothers?'

160

Words such as these are not meant to be interpreted literally, with no consideration of their deeper significance. On an entirely material level they would sound irresponsible, even callous. It is a fact that most prophets and visionaries in the past—as well as the seriously spiritually inclined like Claire today—have discovered it is not easy to exist within society and its expectations.

The spiritual path—even the clear-sightedness of the mystic or visionary—is uncomfortable and intrusive, disturbing to the generally accepted patterns of existence, unwelcome in many people's lives. When motives have to be examined and truths have to be faced—not just one or two little truths that might be lived with reasonably comfortably, but *all* truths—the very sense of self and personal reality by which most people measure their existence is threatened.

Those who accept their 'sight' and increasingly try to live by it become very aware of the boundaries that confine others. There are 'No Go' areas where they can expect to encounter embarrassment, awkwardness or even hostility, not because of anything they do but because of the simple fact that they exist. Their very 'being' is disturbing to some people.

'I wasn't aware as I was growing up that I was "second sighted", "psychic" or whatever you might call it—I just could not understand why people seemed to find me upsetting and why the things I said made them angry,' Claire told me. 'When I was about ten or so, I was taken to visit a relative who was dying of cancer and I did not know what to expect because I had no experience of serious illness. Well, when we went in I saw behind the thinness and pain on her face, a kind of glorious shining—I mean, I really saw it, a wonderful light because her spirit was so purified and strong, and I knew she was almost home, almost free, without knowing how I knew. Without thinking, I smiled at her and said: "Oh, you are so beautiful, so very beautiful. I was afraid but death is a wonderful thing, it is not frightening at all."'

'You can imagine what sort of effect that had on everyone else—but I had no idea I had said anything wrong. I knew that what I had said was true. But my mother scolded me for weeks, so I have never forgotten that particular occasion and there were plenty of others like it.'

'Yes, that kind of outspokenness is something people will accept perhaps in a very young child,' I commented. 'Though even then it might be regarded as embarrassing. Just "Not Done".'

'I couldn't make any sense of it at all—everything I said or did seemed to be "Not Done", and it had nothing to do with whether it was actually real and true or not.' Claire was able to summon a wry smile as she looked back on those difficult years. 'In the end I suppose I stopped being myself—I was obviously unacceptable as I was—so I just acted everything out, the way other people seemed to do it. I watched what everyone else said and did and made sure my reactions were like theirs—because what seemed appropriate to me would always make everyone else angry and embarrassed. I can see, looking back, that it made them rather afraid as well.'

'And now?' I asked.

She sighed. 'It has taken me half a lifetime to stop acting, to feel I can admit to being the real me again. Though even now, knowing and understanding what I do about my "sight", I realise I am never going to be acceptable—not as the "real me"—to a lot of people.'

'That is their problem though, Claire, not yours,' I said. 'You have had to struggle to find your right way, and everyone else will have to find theirs. When they do it, or how, has to be left to them.'

Knowing yourself and being content and at peace with that self is the key to a balanced and happy life. Comparisons are indeed odious. As Brother Gregory might say, do the flowers compare envious notes to see whose colours are brightest, or do the birds suffer from jealousy because one can fly higher or sing more sweetly?

If you are feeling discouraged because the

road you are on seems a hard one and you do not think you are getting very far, remember that there are others who are not even aware there is a road.

CHAPTER EIGHT

PROVISION FOR THE FUTURE

I was conducting a reading on the phone for Rochelle, who lives in London. Having survived several broken relationships she was on her own and finding it lonely. Not surprisingly, she wanted to know when Mister Right—or indeed any sort of acceptable 'Mister' who would brighten her life, would turn up.

Consulting her cards, I assured her that she was about to enter a new relationship at any time.

'Oh, I hope so, but where will I meet him?' she demanded rather despairingly. 'I hardly ever get a chance to get out to meet other people.' I knew that she was an artistic designer and worked from home.

As is always necessary when making any kind of prediction, I could only tell her exactly what I saw. 'You needn't worry about trying to get out and about to meet him. You're not going to meet him by trying. You will just bump into him, I think. Literally. In the street, at the launderette—somewhere.'

But though I secretly thought myself that this all sounded rather vague and unlikely, I was to receive a card a few weeks later from another friend of mine in London who also knew Rochelle. She had written a PS on the back of it.

'Rochelle says to let you know she did bump into him in the street, just as you said!'

On another occasion I was visiting a neighbour, Janet, a very practical lady who hadn't a great deal of time for the world of the spirit. She pushed her hand, palm-upwards, under my nose with the brisk words:

'Read that if you can and tell me whether I will win the Lottery, that's all I want to know about my future.'

Normally I do not deal in specific queries about possible wins or windfalls since the teachings and messages I receive are largely concerned with personal potential and what it can achieve rather than whether one will be able to get a free handout. On this occasion, however, I was able to tell Janet I could see two separate amounts of money heading her way in the near future.

'One will be a small win, probably ten pounds or so,' I told her and she nodded. She had already claimed several previous ten pound wins on the Lottery in the past. 'The other—well, I'm not sure. It may not be a win as such and it certainly won't be a fortune, but I seem to see it being enough to buy something for the home. Probably about two hundred and fifty pounds or thereabouts.'

I did feel that for some reason this second amount was tied to the home though I could not tell Janet in what way. There was little else of interest in her immediate future that I could see, except that when she asked about possible new relationships I told her someone would re-enter her life from the past.

I had forgotten about these predictions when one morning a few weeks later, I met up with Janet's daughter Melanie as she was out walking the dog. She and her mother shared the same flat. They were very close and Melanie had been present when I read her mother's palm.

'We have been meaning to tell you,' she said. 'You know what you said about Mum having two lots of money coming her way? And somebody from the past? Well, she did win a tenner in the Lottery, the next week. And then, guess what? My Dad turned up out of the blue. He and Mum were divorced years ago and we haven't seen him for ages, but he wants to try and make a fresh start—.'

'And don't tell me—he gave your Mum a cash present?' I prompted.

Melanie laughed.

'No, but he gave *me* a present. A present for me and one for Max (her brother). Two hundred and fifty pounds. Each.'

Cases involving prediction—particularly if these have apparently come true—are perhaps the ones that most fascinate people who have little to do with psychic work. Being able to see what lies beyond tomorrow, to catch a glimpse of the untrodden country of the future, this is surely the ultimate in thrilling magic and mystery—which is why there have always been diviners and prophets and there have always been people who were eager to consult them. But though human beings long to see what the future holds they are often afraid of it and want to be reassured that 'Nothing awful will happen to me'—or to my children, or to the ones I love.

In fact, though, it does not take any psychic power to know that this is impossible to guarantee. Some degree of struggle, difficulty and testing as well as the ordinary human trials of existence—loss, pain, grief and so on—comes sooner or later to everyone, and the only certain fact of life is that in the end, we will all die. There is no way that anyone, psychic or not, can undertake to promise that 'Nothing awful will happen'.

At the other extreme I have known cases where sitters will assume a dogged attitude and insist they want to know everything I can see for them in the future 'however bad it is.' In the same way they will view the cards as I turn them over and ask anxiously: 'Is that a good card or a bad one? Don't spare me. If there is something bad ahead, I want to know.'

But there are no 'bad' cards, no 'bad things'

that can ever happen to us in the future, only gateways through which we may need to pass, challenges for us to overcome. The things we may dread and want to hide from or avoid are a necessary part of living, part of the growth process, and whatever the future holds, all experience is there to teach us something if we will let it.

I mentioned at the beginning of this book that my own experiences—many of them extremely painful—did not seem to me to make any sense at the time but now I can see they were part of a pattern. Life is an on-going process, the honing and refining of our spiritual selves. If we refuse to accept this and try to deny the existence of the painful and difficult aspects of living, piling up material security or seeking assurances that there will never be anything unpleasant for us to face up to or cope with, we deny our own spiritual progression, deliberately refuse to allow our souls to develop and mature in wisdom and strength.

It is very necessary to respect the feelings of others—and in my case this includes the fears and anxieties of my sitters. But in my work as a psychic, I will make no catagorical statements one way or the other about whether the future is going to be 'good' or 'bad'. I never assure anyone glibly that 'Nothing awful will happen', but try as we examine their potential future to give them confidence in their own unsuspected strength and ability to overcome whatever problems or adversities they may encounter.

This is the only way in which—whether you know what the future holds or not—you can realistically face it. As a psychic too, I suggest to people that they work to develop faith— whether in just a concept of some higher power or the formal teachings of one of the world's varied belief systems or religions—to help them cope, rather than desperately trying to do everything themselves.

The secret of achieving freedom to live a happy life is to accept whatever the future might bring with a positive attitude. Better than being grimly determined to 'count your blessings' (which can sometimes be an extremely depressing exercise) is to try to maintain a sense of thankfulness and joy in the abundance of the moment rather than look round for something to complain about. To appreciate what you have rather than dwell on what you think you do not have. This is the basic philosophical concept of a system of natural healing called Reiki (which I practise as a Reiki Master). 'Where there is abundance, there can be no lack.'

Needless worrying makes no difference to what is going to happen anyway. The only real kind of insurance against disaster is to know that whatever happens, you have resources you can draw on to confront and deal with it and you will be able to cope somehow and come through.

Originally I had intended to call this chapter *Inspirations for the Future* but as I was in the process of writing it, I found myself suddenly recalling that word 'Provisions' which I had found so cryptic when I encountered the Gatekeeper as I have described in Chapter Two.

I saw suddenly that there is all the difference in the world between loading yourself up with provisions for a journey, stockpiling cumbersome items against all eventualities—and being able to actually enjoy your journey by travelling light. You do not need to carry heavy baggage-loads of provisions into the future but 'provision yourself' mentally so that you are always empowered to obtain whatever might be needed as and when it becomes necessary. This way the journey forward becomes a fun thing, an adventure. And after all, disaster might never strike—the worst might never happen.

The most useful sort of provision for any journey is a map or a book of instructions from some source that can be trusted—preferably someone who has made the journey before you. What one needs is helpful and authoritative words of wisdom. And so far as the journey of life, the journey into the future, is concerned such information is freely available to all in any form of any recognised spiritual teaching—the Bible and the Koran are just two examples.

On a personal level I have also found wisdom and inspiration in the 'channelled' messages and teachings I continue to receive over the years. The extracts I have chosen to include here from 'the Goddess' and Brother Gregory are as simple and as good as bread, refreshing as a drink of fresh water. I hope you will find the same encouragement and inspiration when you read them.

FROM THE GODDESS

When I began to receive 'channelled' texts from 'the Goddess', I naturally started to read and study to find out more about their source. I discovered that in every culture, 'the Goddess' represents the feminine aspect of the Godhead. In the West she is usually identified with the earliest forms of religion which flourished as paganism, Celtic and otherwise. She represents the passive feminine, the Earth, our Mother, Nature in all her forms. The cycles of the months, of the seasons, the necessity for death before rebirth are all Goddess concepts, linked with the mysterious and powerful Moon which rules the secret and feminine side of life.

The Goddess is represented in popular mythology with three faces—the young and lovely Maiden, the mature, nurturing Mother or Lady and the ancient, often repulsive Crone who nevertheless possesses all knowledge and wisdom. These reflect the changing face of woman as she passes through her life and are also expressions of the natural cycles of the Earth itself. They can be frightening in their inevitability, ruthlessly impartial—and immensely beautiful.

The Goddess speaks for the power of the feminine everywhere, for the secrets of womanhood, of birth, death and rebirth, of the existence that is miraculously renewed in the budding of every spring, the stark fact of decay, the passing of all with no exceptions. Everything must pass—and yet everything will be reborn.

It is important to realise that the Goddess is not a feminist concept. In pagan belief, God and Goddess are two halves of the whole, equally necessary and equally powerful in their different ways. The male energies are active, positive, while the female energies are passive, negative. In different symbolism, they are represented as Yin-Yang, Dark-Light, and other such polarised concepts. Together they balance each other. And in fact, the Goddess—as with woman herself—can also seem far more deadly than the God, or the man.

She does not flinch from the reality of things as they are. And if she is cruel, she is also the Mother of all, the presence in the dark which alone will soothe her children to peaceful sleep.

There are innumerable Goddesses who have been worshipped throughout history but they are basically the same one, or aspects of her, simply called by different names. I assumed as my research progressed that I would have to be satisfied for the source of my own personal 'Goddess texts' to remain impersonal, but one day while I was wishing I had an actual name to link them to, someone I could mention to people to make the source more real to them, I opened a book and there she was—her name, Sirona.

It was as though I recognised her from the words that had passed through my mind in the same way one will recognise a person one has spoken to on the phone but not met. I had never heard of this particular Goddess but was able to discover she had been an obscure Romano-Celtic Goddess of healing. Her shrines (there are only one or two known throughout Europe) generally featured healing waters in the form of a pool or spring, and in appearance she was represented with a snake entwined round her wrist, holding in her left hand a bowl containing three eggs to denote fertility.

I was particularly interested in two other descriptive notes concerning her—she was vaguely described as having connections with the stars, and she also had a companion of sorts, a little animal supposedly a type of lapdog. I could not help thinking of my 'Star Plane'—and of the little animal I had encountered there.

ON LOVE

Without love there would be a dark void where the hounds of chaos roam in their packs, baying to the light of a black moon. The strands of love are like the strands of the web spun by the celestial spider that reach across the galaxies, linking planet to planet and the souls of the tiny insects to their counterparts. Love touches like the flake of snow, in its crystalline beauty, which brings stars to rest upon the foreheads of mortal men.

Without love within your heart you are a living corpse, freshly disinterred and with the stink of the grave about you like cere cloths. This is the word of the goddess. The other name for life is love. They are one and the same.

I charge you to love most of all the spirit that is within you. Stoke up the beacon of your self with love until it burns high and clear, and walk the dim corridors of your life with this torch held in your hand so that the red flames may illumine them. Tenderly care for your

175

own spirit, for it is alone in an alien place and in its vulnerability it is to you that it must turn.

Nurture your spirit and love it with complete acceptance of its flaws, for the unsullied, the untouched and the perfect have no place in the struggle for growth. Carry your scars like battle flags and display them proudly, for they are your achievements, and honour your spirit for its victories.

This is the word of the Goddess. Until you can unreservedly love yourself, you have nothing to give to another.

THE MAIDEN

Beneath the arched branches of the willow in the deepest shadow, the maiden lies in sacrifice. Her hands and her feet are bound and her hair dips with the willow branches into the water. Green leaves will mirror her eyes as the spirit of the earth possesses her and fills her; the sounds of the water will drown the gasps of her violated mouth.

For ever it must be so; for ever the maiden must wait in bondage for the spirit to come to her and overshadow her. For ever the water must drown the cries of the virgin and the leaves tremble with the trembling of her body when she is again alone.

The heart of the earth beats fierce and strong, stopping the ears of the virgin. She cannot hide, for all ways lead to the shadow of the green tree and the murmuring of the water. Bind therefore her hands, spread her hair and let her wait for the earth to come to take her for itself.

To the Goddess turn the lost, the bruised and trembling bodies, the bleeding mouths and violated minds. The Goddess is all things to all men. She will bind up the scars and gently soothe the pain of memory, so that once again the leaves are green and not crimson, and once more the water sings and does not weep.

Lay your pain at the feet of the Goddess and she will gladden your heart and lift your soul. Within her glade bloom roses even through the snow, and the nightingale sweetly calls with each rising moon. She brings joy to those who despair and strength to the weak, and illuminates the dark corners of the soul with brightness.

PAST LIFE

Blue the eye of the Goddess and through this gateway streams the light. In a dark land, blue is the colour of the soul and the colour of the water as the river flows, eternal benefactor bringing light and life.

O Isis, in the scrolls of papyri lie the secrets of the palms and the sand, in the lines of destiny and the passage of the caravans across the dunes are forged the links of green and amber, malachite and jade; links of silver and turquoise.

I am the Goddess. I stand for ever in marble and in sandstone, with kohl outlining my eyes so that I see past the present and the future, to the eternal now, which is yet then and to be, and I see into the hearts of men; and the waters stand still in everlasting and perpetual revelation of the truth.

In the shadow of the temple columns glides the white-robed one with gold upon her hair and round her waist, and the blossom of the lotus worked in silks upon the fine linen that whispers with the whisper of her sandals across the floor. She knows the secrets of the inner chamber and passes only when the night is upon the temple with stars, her crown of mystery and magic. Beside her like a ghost, walks the temple cat, whose unblinking regard is of sapphire. She looks with the eyes of the Goddess, for they are one.

And in the snowy mountains where the snow leopard wanders, there too is the shadow of the Goddess, falling dimly upon the snow. Know that even in the burning sands or the green jungle, or the places where the north lights stream their banners, she is there, and in her eye she holds you and will nurture you and keep you, through time and when time has ceased to be.

FROM BROTHER GREGORY

COUNSEL FOR A GARDENER

The world of your inhabiting is a book, my son, use it wisely and learn each day a lesson to help you in your calling. Keep yourself apart from those who would tread the flowers underfoot and lay waste the garden. You have a garden in your keeping, yourself both the gardener and the gatekeeper.

The sun rises and sets, the beetle pursues its ways—these are guidance to the eyes that can read them. The prince lives apart, he does not read with the eye of common man. He has no need of a guide, where would he be guided? He *is*, within his own garden and also a part of it; and the living and the dead, the petals and the leaf-mould are alike known to him. He is not in the restless world but is himself, stillness and calm.

Fireflies and the nightwings of the moth and the voices of the little flowers, these are his companions.

Rest, my son, be still.

COUNSEL FOR A LONELY WOMAN

There is time for growth and for gestation. Do not hurry the force of life, it must move at its own pace; the candle burns hour by hour and

the incense will find its own way upward to
heavens those below cannot see. Hold to the
soft of the dark, the wing of the moth, the
touch of the shadow, the warmth of the breath
held in anticipation, the silence of still winter.
Even in its due course will come the breaking
of the womb, and the light will be a painful
tumult for those who are not ready and
waiting.

Wait, my child, and if necessary wait until
you have passed beyond waiting and the
burden of your awareness has been gently
lifted from you. Oh my child, your own
expectation and your own stillness will reach
out as the ripples on a pond to touch all
around you, therefore your stillness is vital to
those yet at the extreme of the vortex.

Be calm, my child, accept the dark, take it to
you as your long-awaited husband and love the
ignorance and mystery that separate you from
that dark, which is yet a part of yourself.
Accept all, for there is no spitting out of the
pips. You *are*, in perfect wholeness, and your
flaws are flaws only to yourself and your fear.
The apple, the fruit, is a miracle from the hand
of God. So then are you, even in your despair
and degradation, perfect in the eye of the one
who created you.

His touch is sure, his intent purest light,
purest harmony. The sun and moon are your
brother and sister also, the hills are your
strength, the trees will hold out their hands to

clasp your fingers. Oh my child, be aware of your own self, the loveliness of that self in sun and in the flickering of shade, the thundercloud and the shimmering of the rainbow.

Oh child, if you knew the force of the love that watches your every step, that breathes over you and touches your face with an agony of adoration in sleep, that *is* simply because you *are*, you would kneel down in such humility that your forehead would touch the earth.

COUNSEL CONCERNING THE LOSS OF JOY

Sit beside me here in the garden, child, and consider the nature of joy. 'It is nothing,' you tell me, 'and yet without it all the rest is worthless.' Without joy, you say there is no sense of self, no sense of being.

Yet have the flowers joy? Do the yellow-petalled marigolds at the water's edge or the flags with their roots deep in the stream, feel joy? Do not complain that you feel not joy, child, it is the arrogance of smallness within. Joy is there is abundance in the turning of the leaf and the tracery of the clouds. The earth one eminent cathedral swells with joy eternal, who are you that you turn away and tell me you do not feel it?

Perhaps it is so, but the responsibility is yours

and not that of God. Joy is always there, child, the anthem of gloriousness in which you may sing even as the little creatures of the fields, a blind piping and the hiss of weeds that creep low, even those that have no flowers and hide in dark places, they know it and in their way feel joy.

Oh child, you are of this joy, but if you will turn your eyes from the choir and your ears from the shivering notes that crack from hill to hill and shatter the peaks of the mountains, turning rocks to rainbows striding across the valleys, you will indeed experience nothingness. You deny your very self of your own choice, and set yourself apart from the very essence of what *is*. It is not a duty or a struggle to feel joy, child, but the natural state of your being.

Look on the world where death is everywhere and the living creatures pass even in noon gloriousness to dulling of eye and squander of fur and feather, stirred careless by the wind, even the wind that carries with it life. What is death, child, but the darker chord, the bass note of living that must sound beneath the treble, the falling waters and the sun-shimmer of summer.

There is comfort in the deep chords, in the sombreness of the heavy notes and the minor. Take from these, child, and feel the joy of them, yet a deeper joy, a still and silent joy and a pausing in the nimble-footed dance. You are all and yet nothing, you cannot encompass all within yourself, yet even as you surrender the expectation of joy and find joyfulness in the nothing that seems to be, then behold, will not the bleakest wilderness bloom like the rose?

Child, it is so. All is joy, even death, even pain, for is it not all being and existence and the wonder of self-hood? Be, child, and you will be joyful. If you feel no joy, then you have chosen not to be.

COUNSEL CONCERNING THE END

What will the end be?

When I consider this I see only the things I have been taught. The sheaves are gathered for the harvest, the day draws to a close and the abbey bell rings. Is this not enough? Is this not an ending to equal the most bloody vision of Armageddon? Whether a quietness and a peaceful sleep into the grave or in torment, it is still an end.

But only after the day has ended, do there emerge stars.

CHAPTER NINE

ALL SHALL BE WELL

'I don't need to be psychic to tell you what you would wish for if you were given three wishes,' said a middle-aged visitor at one of the Psychic Fairs. 'You'd wish for wealth first.'

'Wrong,' I said.

'You're a fool then. But I know you'd ask for health. You don't need anything if you've got your health.'

'Sorry, wrong again.'

There was a pause.

'You wouldn't want wealth or health? Well, what on earth else could you wish for?'

My three wishes would be for courage to face what I have to, strength to do what I need to, and to be able to accept and endure whatever trials or sufferings I must undergo as cheerfully as I can.

At the end of a sitting, session or reading, before I part from the person who has come to me for help, advice or guidance, I sometimes hand them a book called *A Guide for the Advanced Soul*, the work of Susan Hayward, and ask them to open it at random. This beautiful hand-written book contains quotations, snippets and sayings from many sources and is designed to offer just the right piece of advice or encouragement for anyone at any given time. It is amazing how appropriate these always are, and most sitters really appreciate having their own personal message to take away with them. Sometimes the messages are tough, sometimes practical, sometimes inspiring—whatever the situation calls for.

I would like to end this book with some similar words for you to take away with you. My three wishes might sound pessimistic, but in fact it is only when one is prepared to accept the worst that one stops being afraid of it. And when you stop being afraid of your enemy, it stops being an enemy.

Whatever the future holds for us all, whether pollution causes smoking and cars to be banned from our cities, whether the damage to the Ozone Layer causes a new Ice Age, whether developing viruses threaten to wipe out the human race through epidemics and plagues—whatever is to happen, there is always hope. It was the visionary Julian of Norwich who assured us that: *All shall be well and all manner of thing shall be well.*

In the end, the final decision is not ours to make. And it is always the simple things—the blooming of a flower, the song of a bird—that triumphantly survive and endure while great civilisations come and go. We can only do what we can, try our best and then leave the rest to that higher power.

I often find that it is the sitters who consult me about what they should be doing or offering or contributing, who are the ones already doing far more than their share. I have encountered many apparently successful, powerful men and women—including heads of business, lawyers and even a judge, film and television producers and personalities, icons of the fashion world, one 'incognito' world sports star, bankers and financiers, writers, designers, even top psychics. Many of them have been just as vulnerable as those who have not been so successful or famous, and have needed the reassurance that it would all come right, the encouragement to believe in themselves and go on.

We all have our own particular battles to fight, but out of struggle and suffering we emerge purified, cleansed, refined and with new wisdom, new enlightenment. In many religions, initiates are set tasks they must perform, tortures they must endure, demons they must overcome. Those who would reach the highest spiritual levels must cross the frontiers of living and dying, face the dark and the light, pass the limits of fear, go out into the void and return.

I can only speak for myself. As a human being, I know one never stops being afraid, and that keeping the faith is a constant challenge. But we can all transcend ourselves if we try and if we believe.

At the beginning of my psychic career, Richard told me that I had 'Egyptian gold' in my aura (the sheath surrounding the physical body, in which some psychics can see and interpret colours). I liked the sound of 'Egyptian gold' and asked what it meant. The answer was even better.

'Ancient wisdom.'

Delightful! But the colours of the aura change according to one's state of physical health and spiritual progress or lack of it, and on another occasion, when I wanted to be cheered up and I asked what he saw in my aura, he answered unflatteringly:

'Muddy brown.'

When I asked the source from which my strength and wisdom comes for a message of my own, a personal 'quote' to take with me to encourage me and guide me as a psychic, as an 'interpreter', and just as myself, this was what I received.

The mountains of the moon are desolate and empty, and there are holes in time where the past was, and is no longer. Those who were shining, shine no more and their shadows exist only, no substance to cast those shadows.

Now their truth must be spoken through you.

Speak your truth always, and that is enough.

187

We hope you have enjoyed this Large Print book. Other Chivers Press or Thorndike Press Large Print books are available at your library or directly from the publishers.

For more information about current and forthcoming titles, please call or write, without obligation, to:

Chivers Press Limited
Windsor Bridge Road
Bath BA2 3AX
England
Tel. (01225) 335336

OR

Thorndike Press
P.O. Box 159
Thorndike, Maine 04986
USA
Tel. (800) 223-2336

All our Large Print titles are designed for easy reading, and all our books are made to last.